Recommendations from readers:

"Over the years, I have learned to listen to the advice given by Linda Schurman. She has demonstrated time and again that her analysis and insights into world affairs and trends is consistently accurate. On a personal level, because of her, I moved my retirement monies out of the stock market into fixed income investments and made money. At that time, many of my colleagues who had not done so lost almost half of their investments."

Claire Kenna, M.B.A., Software Engineer

"We are living in the midst of a chaotic tipping point of human civilization. We could choose to go forth blindly guessing, clinging to past strategies, or get informed about the currents that are in play well into the future. There is no better time than now to have maps to guide our choices. Linda's book is a cautionary examination of the 'cosmic weather' and the choices we have available to us as a society and as individuals. I have been consulting with Linda since 1976. Her predictions have prepared me to comprehend the challenges that lie ahead – like bringing an umbrella when rain is in the forecast."

Hina Pendle, PhD, hina@uspartners.com

"Linda Schurman correctly predicted the financial downturns of this decade back in the 1990s. She has an amazing track record in predicting the geopolitical upheavals we are currently experiencing. She successfully combines information from global financial, political and scientific sources with historical research and future planetary placements, to create not only a startling picture of our future, but point the way to humanity's creation of a world that can work for all its inhabitants."

James H. Cook, PhD, Legal Consultant

I

"Having followed Linda's predictions for more than three decades, I am in awe of her uncanny, almost eerie accuracy. In her first book, 'What Next? A Survival Guide to the 21st Century', Linda lovingly and meticulously unfolds the challenges we will (and have now begun) to face, coupled with practical advice for positioning ourselves to cope with them. Who could deny the series of very recent wake up calls that have affected almost every aspect of our lives?...from our wallets, to the fragile roofs over our heads, to the very air we breathe, not to mention those wonderful electronic gadgets and social media, that when the power goes off, become just plastic and wires, leaving us feeling alone and isolated.

Linda now graces us with 'Fast Forward -- Surviving the Race to the Future'. Read it once, read it twice, take notes and take action. Her predictions, which I am certain will come true, at first blush rattled me to the core. Then I read it again and focused on what could be. Fear morphed to hope. Her practical advice...so many great ideas and wonderful references, are a true guide to coping with what will surely come. Read it once, read it twice..."

Kathy Spiliotopoulos, Business Entrepreneur and Health Care Consultant

Fast Forward

Surviving the Race to the Future

By Linda Schurman

I wish to dedicate this book to my husband, Richard, whose support, in every way, has made this book possible.

I wish to convey my sincere appreciation to Linda Lane of Lazerlady Publishing for her encouraging me every step of the way to continue writing about where my passion lies; to do my best to pursue the truth and share these efforts with my readers.

I also wish to thank my cherished friend Mayraj Fahim, who has supplied me with so many excellent sources of information, including the works of "truth-telling" journalists and authors. Without her help, constructing and documenting my books would have been much more difficult.

Fast Forward

Fast Forward

paperback ISBN: 978-0-9796900-1-3
epub ISBN: 978-0-9796900-3-7
Library of Congress Control Number: 2012953728

Lazer Lady Publishing, Inc.
P.O. Box 812742
Wellesley, MA 02482

lazerladypublishing.com

LINDA SCHURMAN

Introduction

A definition of astrology: A study of the timing and the meaning of astronomical events in relationship to historic themes and issues that arise in our lives here on earth.

THE challenges human beings face today are enormous; perhaps the greatest since the dawn of human civilization over 5,200 years ago when the Egyptians, and Babylonians were moving from nomadic tribal existences into agricultural nation states ruled by warrior kings. Interestingly, the end of the "long count" which began August 11, 3114 B.C.E. in the Mayan Calendar falls on the Winter Solstice, December 21st of 2012.   There is evidence that the end of the first "long count" coincided with a catastrophe, possibly an asteroid collision with earth that ended Bronze Age civilizations such as the Sumerians.

Our mass media has been filled with dire predictions about what this all means, including "the end of the world", a pole shift, the collapse of our civilization (a fate the Maya suffered), "the rapture", "the return of Jesus Christ", the return of the Hindu God Krishna, and the landing of aliens from other galaxies.

In my last book, "What Next? A Survival Guide to the 21st Century", published in June of 2007, I made a series of predictions that few people wanted to hear, i.e. a crisis in the global economy accompanied by a great depression, serious repercussions of climate change resulting in weather extremes, a cycle of increasingly intense earthquakes and volcanic activity, and energy and environmental destruction precipitating movements to end the age of oil and fossil fuels. My thesis was, and still is, that we can modify and therefore change our fate by being willing to face the truths of our existence and step up to the plate to invent our way out of the historic crises that are now seemingly engulfing us.   In this spirit, this book has not been written specifically for astrologers, (astrological charts are printed in the back of this book), but its purpose is to translate what the planetary patterns have to say to all of us.

Here in the United States, I think most of us would agree, our political and industrial leaders are seriously failing to rescue our society on all levels. There is a lack of compassion, imagination, and, most of all, the will to stand up for the greater good. In fact the term "greater good" has been subsumed by a number of powerfully placed individuals characterized by self-absorption and a ruthless grabbing and hoarding of the world's capital and resources who operate out of a small number of trans-national corporations, giant banks and transnational coal, gas, and oil corporations. Recently, the "too big to fail" financial institutions were bailed out by the U.S. government and its tax payers, while millions of Americans lost their jobs, housing, access to advanced education, and life savings. These same highly positioned elites are the ones who are paying for the campaigns of our elected officials, own many of the media outlets that dominate the discourse in the nation, and are co-opting the very essentials we need to survive; our lands, our natural resources, and our waters.

Like the Roman Empire before us, the U.S. government is draining our national treasure in wars with foreign nations that did not attack us, so that we can control resources; oil and gas pipelines and their strategic waterways. Since the 1970s, manufacturing has essentially left the U.S. taking its jobs to nations with a cheap labor force and no environmental laws. The economy has thus become "financialized" , creating an enormously wealthy class who "game" the system, and eroding and diminishing much of what was referred to as the "middle class".

This is indeed the "dark night of the soul" in America and in many other parts of the world who have virtually abandoned their higher instincts and greater perspectives. This same group of nations continues to exploit the environment, to expand their unrelenting use of fossil fuels, and to consume products and resources until the fate of the Easter Islanders overtakes them and us. Recently, Super Storm Sandy devastated New York City and New Jersey coastal regions and has fulfilled the prediction of climate scientists concerning the consequences of global climate change. Surely, it would seem, the end of the world, as we have conceived it, is just over the horizon.

What do the Constellations say?

On December 21, 2012, for the first time in about 26,000 years, the sun rises to conjunct the intersection of the plane of the ecliptic and the Milky Way. The Winter Solstice points to the center of the galaxy at about 27 degrees of the constellation Sagittarius.

I have spent the larger part of my life studying astronomical events and their relationship to cycles and occurrences in human history. As an astrologer, I have witnessed the unfolding of the challenges, themes, and opportunities the planets foretell. I feel it is my mission to present the issues of our times so that we may come face to face with the critical on-the-ground realities that are here with us in the present and are challenging us in ways that are nearly incomprehensible as we move into the future. This is not the time to anesthetize ourselves by denying factual information or looking the other way.

Surprisingly, however, these very challenging times may present to us an atmosphere in which a grand evolutionary leap in human consciousness becomes possible. Rising beyond the primitive mindless exploitation of the earth and one another, we may move into a human expression of intelligence, compassion and spiritual understanding beyond anything we ever imagined.

It is entirely probable that the realities of our prior history could fade into irrelevance as we discover a new form of nearly limitless energy that has nothing to do with fossil fuel. As many of the most powerful and abusive are toppled, we may rediscover local, effective, grass roots democracy, worker-owned and operated entrepreneurial businesses, sustainable agriculture, solar architecture, and a satisfying connection with family and community. Most of all, we may actually feel an inner resonance with all life on earth; an elevation of spirit within new frameworks of consciousness that comprise what we are yet to become.

Table of Contents

LINDA SCHURMAN

Chapter 1

Into the Great Revolution – Politics, Science, Energy

Uranus in Aries (March 12, 2011 – March 5, 2019),
(Square Pluto 2011 – 2016)
(Last transited Aries 1927 – 1934)

Uranus in Taurus (March 7, 2019 – July 6, 2025)
(Last transited Taurus 1934 – 1942)

Uranus is a planet whose symbolism and mythology is associated with the "wow" factor. Its astrological meaning is associated with experiences leading to sudden personal transformations and the emergence of innovations that forever change the tide of history. It appears to coincide with extremes of fate, ranging from lightening striking a building and burning it to the ground, to a multitude of grand and exciting technological breakthroughs such as the discovery and application of electricity, nuclear energy, air and space travel, rocketry, quantum physics, computers and the internet. Uranus was discovered in 1781 around the time of the American Revolution, the French Revolution, and the Industrial Revolution, ushering these ideas fully into the collective consciousness of many nations and societies who were rising into positions of power in the world.

A key to this planet's archetypal psychological profile lies in the Greco/ Roman legends. They tell us that Uranus was a god so afraid of being "unseated" that he devoured his own children to hold onto his power. The mythic narrative goes on to tell us that his son Saturn managed to escape, defeat and kill his father, and release his siblings.

Uranus also has some historical association with Prometheus, who is said to have brought the great gift of fire to humanity, and was punished severely for this by the gods. Thus, Uranus's symbolism in astrological lore is one of the "loner", the isolated genius whose scientific discoveries liberate humankind, but whose eccentricities border on fanaticism. He is behind grand revolutions and the overthrow of the existing hierarchy of ruling elites. He prefers the "ideal of democracy and personal freedom", abhors authority and tyranny, but does not necessarily guarantee replacing the old order with a cohesive, workable system.

The present transit of Uranus in Aries:

This is the era when disillusioned young people all over the world are looking at the elite elders and their leaders who have constructed a transnational global economy where the upper one to two per cent of the population own or control eighty to ninety per cent of the world's wealth. They have observed their parents' and grandparents' generations benefit from an unprecedented series of technological and democratically based economic opportunities since the end of WW II. They have also witnessed a human population expansion to around seven billion people and growing. Most of this enormous industrial enlargement and human population expansion was made possible by unprecedented quantities of energy generated by coal, oil, uranium, and gas. The result of these historic decisions and events is a virtually unrestrained usage and consumption of everything from water, farm land, fossil fuels, and minerals, nearly to the point of exhaustion and polluting the environment to almost incomprehensible levels.

The young are taking a sad look at generations of corporate heads, who have financed the campaigns of politicians who have succumbed to temptation and allowed these corporations to take of control of our political agendas. The companies that perceive employees as "enemies of profits", are motivated to move all over the globe to hire the poorest and least powerful people for whom they can pay the least and to locations that are tax free. By doing this, they dismantle tax-financed local infrastructures and societies that support the very existence of civilization itself. In addition, there has been an ensuing but inevitable replacement of human labor with high tech machinery and robots doing the work people used to do. The current result has been even though we have every conceivable electronic device, the internet, and global communications networks, these young people are looking at unemployment, unaffordable education, and a general dimming of their dreams. In addition to witnessing the disappearance of a middle class, people-at-large are also seeing the dissolving of what made America great in the first place: the ideals of democracy and equal opportunity.

In decades gone by, there have been "reforms" instituted in the "Welfare" system in an attempt to help poor people become more independent and get to work. There have been people who "worked" the system at public expense. Today, about half of America is on some kind of public assistance; not because they want to be there, but have little or no choice. We need to realize that "public assistance" is not just welfare, but includes food stamps, unemployment insurance, Medicare, Medicaid, and Social Security Disability and Social Security for retirement.

In an article published on October 3, 2012 in Common Dreams.org, the subject was an interview with Der Spiegel of Nobel economist, Joseph Stiglitz . "noted Columbia University economist and 2001 Nobel Prize winner Joseph Stiglitz says that 'the American dream has become a myth'. . . . Stiglitz highlights the inequality in the U.S. that has grown 'dramatically' as wealth is concentrated in the upper echelon because the 'marvelous economic machine' in the U.S. reinforces the division."

Even more alarming, they are witnessing the development of a surveillance police state licensed to penetrate the affairs of every U.S. citizen through the passage of and extension of The Patriot Act and a series of laws recently passed that clearly violates the constitution by allowing the military to detain citizens without due process, and places severe limits on our traditional rights to protest. Specifically, the National Defense Authorization Act makes it legal for the military to capture and detain citizens without "due process". The Federal Restricted Buildings and Grounds Improvement Act restricts our constitutional right to peacefully protest. The National Defense Resources Preparedness Act authorizes the President and cabinet officials to take over crucial parts of the U.S. economy, not just in national emergencies, but in peacetime.

Many of our young men and women are currently still engaged in a costly war in Afghanistan, the longest engagement in our history, much of which is about the control of vast natural resources; oil, gas, and water, that are being used up as developing nations are demanding access to greater and greater volumes of these deposits. The present administration in Washington has promised we will be "out" by 2014. However, the U.S. government seems to be undergoing a shift in the way it wages war by using secret "special ops forces" and drones to penetrate sovereign nations' territories to bomb terrorist cells, and often killing innocent bystanders in the process.

Our media's obsession with the end of the Maya calendar "long count" is likely a subconscious projection of all our fears; that the end of life on earth is near; that, like the Maya, we may succumb to over-population and consumption of resources to the point of the collapse of our civilization.

The young and the restless:

As Uranus entered Aries in March of 2011, a sign associated with youth, energy, innovation, the world witnessed the "Arab Spring" in which young people began their revolutions, challenging despotic government leaders in Tunisia, Egypt, Libya, Syria, Yemen, with stirrings elsewhere in the Middle Eastern states. It should give us pause to reflect that, ironically, these revolutions are taking place in the part of the world where civilization began about 5200 years ago, the beginning of the last Maya long count.

The internet and its newly developed social networking matrices were a significant factor in their successful unseating of local despots. Many people here in the U.S. felt admiration for the courage these young people exhibited against these totalitarian regimes and their standing military complexes that are associated with the planet Pluto (concentrated power). However, the process of electing their "ideal" replacements has, so far, eluded them since religious sects continue to line up against one another.

As the harsh realities of our economic depression here and in Europe manifest, severe weather disasters, fluctuating oil prices, unemployment, the crash of the housing market, are staring us in the face. Many young people are overwhelmed, disoriented, and seem to be "at sea" with little or no direction. Others are realizing they must make a fundamental change in direction that encompasses living in concert with life on earth and in cooperation with each other. This collective shift in consciousness consisting of working together for a shared prosperity, would likely move humankind away from its destruction and toward its salvation.

The Second American Revolution

Here in the U.S., the Occupy Wall Street Movement began on September 17, 2011 in New York City,   taking a public stand against inequality and economic abuses by the upper 1% in wealth, and using the tool of peaceful protest.   One of the most constructive outgrowths of this public stance is a proposed constitutional amendment to take all private money out of all political campaigns. Another positive outgrowth is this organization calling attention to the loss of funding and breakdown of civil society and its infrastructure, resulting in increased losses of jobs, housing, schools and everything that supports a middle class in our society.

Aries can be violent, warlike, impatient, self-absorbed, and clueless about the consequences of the actions it takes. This new energy needs to be focused rather than scattered. It needs templates, projects, and assemblages of people who are passionate about a better future and a brighter world. It will take a lot more than tweeting or texting. It will require of us that we move beyond the age of mechanistic materialism and mass consumption into an age of living in concert with life on earth and in cooperation with each other.

We need to develop new economic models that employ people in sustainable industries in smart wired cities and prosperous villages whose network technologies are generated from a grass roots democratic base rather than imposed from the top down. We need young entrepreneurs in worker owned businesses, whose sole motivation is not greed, but to generate a mutual prosperity founded on reversing human damage to the earth's ecology that has led to the greatest extinction of species since the dinosaurs went down. We need to re-localize our efforts into "grass roots" smaller ecologically designed communities where democracy is not isolated but closer at hand.

Wellesley, Massachusetts has assembled a recycling center that, for 25 years, is one of the most comprehensive in the U.S. and earns an additional $500,000 per year for the city. Intentional communities, including eco villages are going up in the U.S. and around the globe, emphasizing living sustainably in a green environment and meeting the challenges of solving problems as community without running anyone over or leaving anyone behind. Later in this book, I will illustrate these models in greater detail.

As before, we may be embarking upon a new series of "revolutions"; the Green Revolution, the New Energy Revolution, and the Democratic Economy Revolution.

A New Energy to Power the World

Pluto was "discovered" in 1930, as the Great Depression took hold in the U.S. In Germany, the rise of Hitler and the Nazis led to the Third Reich and the advent of World War II. The last time Pluto was square Uranus in Aries (April 1932 – March 1933), as the failed economy threatened to dismantle America, Franklin D. Roosevelt was nominated for the presidency, promising his famous "New Deal", and won on November 8th.

Amidst this harsh period, an astounding development occurred that most people ignored. On May 1, 1932, physicists performed a successful experiment in London, splitting the atom. On January 8, 1933, American physicist Dr. Irving Langmuir measured the force of a single atom. These discoveries led us into the atomic age as the trajectory begun in the early part of the 20th Century with the advent of quantum theory gave birth to successful experimentation. We all now know that later on, this led to the Manhattan Project and our development of the atomic bomb dropped on Japan in 1945, ending WW11. Later, nuclear energy was developed for peaceful uses and nuclear plants were built, supplying power to nations all over the world. Recently, since the disasters from Three Mile Island to Chernobyl to Fukushima, we are painfully aware of the deadly hazards of radiation and the dire consequences of nuclear facility leaks and meltdowns. The search for nuclear fusion, a process whereby no pollution is generated has gone on for years, to no avail until now.

Presently, Uranus is square Pluto once again until early 2016. This is a longer period than the previous one that, in some ways, will likely extend our period of economic suffering, but in other ways may symbolize major breakthroughs in physics and energy production.

In the (2011) September 9th "Mail Online" newsletter, it was announced: "Britain has joined forces with America to investigate a hi-tech new way of producing clean energy – not from wind or waves, but from firing huge arrays of high-powered lasers at pellets of hydrogen. Recent experiments at America's National Ignition Facility have produced huge bursts of energy from the technology – using a stadium-sized building housing an array of 192 lasers which fire a 500 terrawatt flash at a drop of hydrogen atoms just 1 mm across". At a meeting recently of London's Royal Society, David Willits, the UK's Science Minister stated, "This is an absolutely classic example of the connections between really high-grade theoretical scientific research and a fundamental human need: our energy supply." In the experiment in September, a burst of power was released from the fusion reaction that was equivalent to the world's entire energy consumption.

We have a long way to go before an infrastructure for this is in place and hydrogen fusion is not without controversy. In the June Issue 2012 of Scientific American (pp. 58-61), reporter Geoff Brumfiel wrote an article entitled "Fusion's Missing Pieces", reporting on ITER (formerly the International Thermonuclear Experimental Reactor) built by six countries and the European Union to create fusion and solve the world's energy and environmental crises. Delays, disappointments, and snafus have plagued their efforts, and it is worth reading the article that describes the challenges inherent in this project. What interests me is that the "start date" for the plant has been moved to late 2020, when the Jupiter/Saturn conjunction takes place in Aquarius and marks the end of this depression cycle. He states "The first real energy-producing experiments will not come before 2026 – two decades after the start of construction." 2024-2026 are the dates I project for the "limitless supply of energy that is not fossil fuel" to be ready for use as Pluto enters Aquarius and is sextile Neptune in Aries and trine Uranus in Gemini. I have made this prediction multiple times in my online newsletters. Transportation, manufacturing, and communication industries have their energy problems solved as the age of fossil fuels goes into obsolescence.

As I am writing this book, the announcement that the famous Higgs Boson particle's existence has been substantiated by the scientists at CERN in Geneva, Switzerland.

The press release took place on the U.S. birthday, July 4th 2012 and has happened just as Pluto and Uranus have formed their exact square. This is called the "God Particle" because its function is to allow atomic particles to organize themselves into matter, creating what we call the Universe. This discovery has such monumental implications for changing our view of reality, we can hardly conceive of the knowledge and understanding of our existence this may unleash. Pluto will continue to be square Uranus through early 2016.

The technology for hydrogen fuel cells is evolving quickly into what is affordable and feasible. The problem here has been that in order to release hydrogen, fossil fuel is needed. This issue is currently being addressed and solutions may be in sight. Each building could have all its energy needs met with an installed hydrogen fuel cell that could be purchased or leased.

BATTERY TECHNOLOGY is progressing rapidly, that would solve energy storage problems connected with windmills, solar panels, and the building of electric autos that could go over 600 miles without needing to be recharged. Private companies are working with Cornell University research labs to develop a battery that is about 95% efficient, contrasted to current batteries that are, at the most, about 19% efficient. Most recently, it was announced that Germany, as the result of the Fukishima nuclear disaster in Japan, is launching a major effort to create a sustainable energy matrix to power their nation without the use of nuclear plants. They are currently supplying large amounts of energy through a combination of solar panels and windmills, defying the predictions of the "naysayers" who have said it cannot be done.

Huge amounts of energy could be saved with proper construction of buildings, using "PASSIVE" ARCHITECTURE. This "house within a house" design is being used or considered in eco-villages throughout the U.S. There are materials available that are so insulating that the interior of the building maintains a constant temperature of about 57-60 degrees year round, needing no central heat. These houses have been built in Germany, Canada, Sweden, Denmark, Finland and Norway. Too few of these have been built in the U.S., but movements are afoot to do so. Housing with south-facing windows, solar- collecting walls and highly effective insulation, combined with specific landscaping are all energy conserving solutions. In my first book, "What Next? A Survival Guide to the 21st Century", solar architect Donna Musial wrote an essay describing how to accomplish these objectives.

SOLAR TECHNOLOGY is progressing rapidly. China is, to date, the largest producer of solar panels that are frequently developed by American engineers. Solar applications are being built all over the world. This is a winning combination with WIND POWER, and can be a pathway to sustainable green energy. Combined with the use of near- perfect batteries that store power when there is no sun or wind, this will soon become viable.

There will obviously be more than one pathway to energy conservation and production, but we are at a threshold we must cross over. The rapid cannibalization of our planet for fossil fuels is threatening not only the global climate, but the basic health of our oceans which is the foundation for all life on earth. The explosion and eruption of oil in the BP catastrophe in the Gulf in 2010 (which I predicted in my online newsletter, www.soothesayer. com)) is only one in a series of pipeline leaks and spills. A similar explosion recently occurred at a drilling operation about 300 miles off the coast of Brazil. Currently, the U.S., China, India, Brazil are all developing giant undersea drilling operations all over the world, including (except the U.S.) off the shores of Cuba where recently some of the largest deposits of undersea oil have been discovered. A severe accident of the magnitude of the BP eruption could threaten the State of Florida and the ecological health of the entire region. In addition to all this, both the U.S. and Russia are battling over a land grab in the arctic to drill for oil and gas in a region whose melting ice is threatening the release of methane gas into the atmosphere that creates the most intense heat of all the greenhouse gasses.

Global Tectonics

Something that is seldom examined or mentioned is the effect that these drilling operations may have on undersea global tectonics. I have predicted in my previous book and newsletters that we are in a major cycle of earthquake and volcanic activity, especially in the period between 2010 through 2016. Already, we have had an increase in numbers and severity of tectonic activity around the world. Recently, clusters of earthquakes have been occurring in Arkansas, Kansas, and Oklahoma near sites that contain "fracking" operations for natural gas. In 2010, we witnessed the twice eruption of an Icelandic volcano and a series of major earthquakes in Haiti and Chile. In March 2011, a giant 9.00 earthquake accompanied by a catastrophic tsunami hit Japan, releasing radio active cesium from its Fukushima nuclear plants that has travelled across the Pacific Ocean to Northern California. Mt. Tongarine in New Zealand erupted (not active for 100 years) and there was a serious earthquake in Christ Church that evoked massive destruction of the city. On Aug. 21, 2012, Mt. Tungurahua erupted in Ecuador. In April of 2012, a volcano erupted near Mexico City causing large-scale evacuations. In June 2012, a 5.7 on the Richter Scale earthquake occurred in Southern China, displacing nearly 100,000 people. In October 2012, a massive earthquake , the strongest in 54 years occurred in Canada which dried up their famous Haida Gwaii Hot Springs. There are always small earthquakes around the world, but the recent occurrences are more serious and seem to be escalating in frequency.

I am attaching a map of earthquakes recorded for seven days in late October 2012 through early November. An astonishing 325 earthquakes took place in this time frame.

This website is available to the public on the government website USGS, http://earthquake.usgs.gov/earthquakes/map.

We need to at least ask ourselves the question: In addition to normal tectonic cycles, could the oceanic drilling and inland "fracking" operations be partially contributing to geological instability, to contamination of our water supplies inland and threatening the complex hierarchies of life in the world's oceans.

Global Climate Change: the Elephant in the room:

There have been many debates with regard to global warming and greenhouse gas emissions produced by humankind past, present, and future.

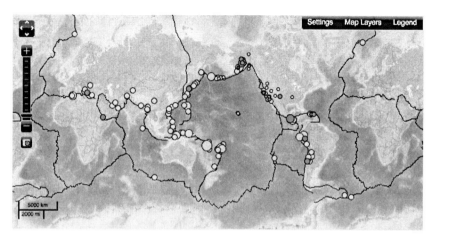

This issue has, unfortunately, become highly politicized and polarizing. On January 27, 2012 an op-ed article was printed in the Wall Street Journal entitled, "No Need to Panic About Global Warming" signed by sixteen scientists. On Feb. 1, 2012, thirty-nine scientists responded with an essay also published in the Wall Street Journal. Since this is concise and comprehensive, I am quoting this letter in its entirety.

" Do you consult your dentist about your heart condition? In science, as in any area, reputations are based on knowledge and expertise in a field and on published, peer-reviewed work. If you need surgery, you want a highly experienced expert in the field who has done a large number of the proposed operations.

You published "No Need to Panic About Global Warming" (op-ed Jan. 27) on climate change by the climate-science equivalent of dentists practicing cardiology. While accomplished in their own fields, most of these authors have no expertise in climate science. The few authors who have such expertise are known to have extreme views that are out of step with nearly every other climate expert. This happens in nearly every field of science. For example, there is a retrovirus expert who does not accept that HIV causes AIDS. And it is instructive to recall that a few scientists continued to state that smoking did not cause cancer, long after that was settled science.

Climate experts know that the long-term warming trend has not abated in the past decade. In fact, it was the warmest decade on record. Observations show unequivocally that our planet is getting hotter. And computer models have recently shown that during periods when there is a smaller increase of surface temperatures, warming is occurring elsewhere in the climate system, typically in the deep ocean. Such periods are a relatively common climate phenomenon, are consistent with our physical understanding of how the climate system works, and certainly do not invalidate our understanding of human-induced warming or the models used to simulate that warming.

Thus, climate experts also know what one of us, Kevin Trenberth, actually meant by the out-of-context, misrepresented quote used in the op-ed. Mr. Trenberth was lamenting the inadequacy of observing systems to fully monitor warming trends in the deep ocean and other aspects of the short-term variations that always occur, together with the long-term human-induced warming trend.

The National Academy of Sciences of the U.S. (set up by President Abraham Lincoln to advise on scientific issues), as well as major national academies of science around the world and every other authoritative body of scientists active in climate research have stated that the science is clear: The world is heating up and humans are primarily responsible. Impacts are already apparent and will increase. Reducing future impacts will require significant reductions in emissions of heat-trapping gases.

Research shows that more than 97% of scientists actively publishing in the field agree that climate change is real and human caused. It would be an act of recklessness for any political leader to disregard the weight of evidence and ignore the enormous risks that climate change clearly poses. In addition, there is very clear evidence that investing in the transition to a low-carbon economy will not only allow the world to avoid the worst risks of climate change, but could also drive decades of economic growth. Just what the doctor ordered."

Threatened Oil, Peak Water, and Running Out:

Nations in the Middle East are coming apart at the seams. With revolutionary Uranus transiting in Aries since March of 2011, civil wars and the overthrow of oppressive regimes there will likely continue to destabilize the area, threatening the supply lines of oil and keeping global oil prices high. Recent fears of Iran developing a nuclear weapon have brought about Israel and the U.S. embargoes and pressures and Iran's threats to close down the Gulf of Hormuz. In addition, there is a rivalry escalating between Saudi Arabia, a Sunni Muslim nation, and Iran, a Shiite Muslim nation. With the civil war in Syria threatening to depose the Assad regime, Iran is losing its only ally. The fighting of these same factions of Islam is currently tearing apart Iraq. Threats to the flow of oil to the rest of the world through Bab el-Mandab (the strait located near Yemen connecting to the Red Sea to the Gulf of Aden) are lesser known, but equally serious. Iran supplies electricity to portions of Afghanistan and we are committed to our military exiting there in 2014. Afghanistan's Taliban inhabits border areas in Pakistan. Between now and 2016, serious conflicts are symbolized in the chart of Iran. Iran's chart is being seriously activated in the spring of 2013 by eclipses and transiting Saturn in Scorpio. This entire area is a "mine field" of possible turmoil and concentration of U.S. enmity.

After nearly nine years of war and occupation, in 2011, U.S. troops left Iraq, ending the multi-trillion dollar war there. A new book has recently been published by author Greg Muttit; "Fuel on the Fire: Oil and Politics in Occupied Iraq" that describes how big transnational oil companies were behind all this and the consequential devastation of the Iraqi people. In an article printed on TomDispatch.com Aug. 27, 2012, he writes: "Here, as a start, is a little scorecard of what's gone on in Iraq since Big Oil arrived two and a half years ago: corruption's skyrocketed; two Western oil companies are being investigated for either giving or receiving bribes; the Iraqi government is paying oil companies a per-barrel fee according to wildly unrealistic production targets they've set, whether or not they deliver that number of barrels; contractors are heavily over-charging for drilling wells, which the companies don't mind since the Iraqi government picks up the tab." He goes on to report: " Iraqis still have an average of just five hours of electricity a day, which in 130 degree heat causes tempers to boil over regularly. The country's two great rivers, the Tigris and Euphrates, which watered the cradle of civilization 5,000 years ago are drying up." It is worth reading his article and his book which extensively cover the insidious motivations of the Bush administration and the disastrous consequences for Iraq. The story is far from over.

The Bakkan Oil Fields in Canada and the Western U.S.A. are bringing in significant new supplies, plus drilling technology has evolved to dig ever deeper into the ground and off shore in deeper and deeper parts of the oceans. Ironically, America is becoming the "energy capitol" of the world. All this would seem to alleviate concerns about running out of oil and gas. But terrible explosions like the BP disaster in the Gulf of Mexico and off the coast of Brazil, and earthquakes occurring in sites where "fracking" for natural gas and digging for oil point to hazards in the environment we may never have considered. With all this increase in access to oil and gas, we are still not meeting the escalating demand on a worldwide basis which is rapidly exceeding supplies. What many Americans do not realize is that much of our oil and gas is being piped across the nation to the Gulf of Mexico by transnational Big Oil and sold directly to India and China. The oil companies are concerned about profits; not whether or not the U.S. is "energy self sufficient".

Water and Soil – The Necessities of Life:

Exploding populations coupled with glaciers melting in mountains that have supplied aquifers in locations throughout the world, are creating serious scarcity of potable water without which we cannot live. This includes the rapidly decreasing eastern Himalayan glaciers that have provided fresh water to India and China for thousands of years. We have also exhausted soil with the practice of industrialized farming, and the use of genetically modified (GM) seeds that use up larger amounts of water, and invite contamination with the use of weed killers that they have been programmed to "resist". Corporate agriculture is also creating food "monocultures" that threaten extinction to a single species if a particular infestation targets it. For the past decade, there has been an alarming dying out of bee populations upon whom the whole world depends for pollination of crops. The (2012) March 31st issue of "Common Dreams. org" published an article entitled "Neurotoxic Pesticides.." that sited several important scientific papers showing deadly effects of neurotoxic pesticides called Newonicotinoids, applied to seeds that permeate the plants. When the pollinators land on the plants, they absorb this chemical that makes them weak and unable to complete their long journeys back to their colonies. Thus the colonies die out. Practices of industrialized farming with immediate profit as their primary motive may be posing multiple threats to our delicately balanced eco-systems. The recent climate extremes from flooding to drought (the worst in 50 years in the U.S.) bring to the forefront of our awareness the delicate balances of nature.

History has taught us over and over again that terrible wars break out when resources become scarce. Today's weapons technologies surpass anything ever contemplated by humankind in the past. Will we invent new sources of energy and launch programs of mass conservation or will we invent new weapons of mass destruction? It will be one of these choices. Our voices need to be heard by those Plutocrats who are resisting the overthrow of the existing order, protecting their enormous personal profiteering, and ensuring their stranglehold on power in governments throughout the world. The time has gone when we could wait passively on the sidelines and do nothing. I think we can rise to this monumental occasion.

The breakthroughs in energy mentioned above could bring an end to the dominance of institutions supporting Big Oil with its huge government subsidies and ensuing environmental devastation. It could bring an end to the Western invasions in the Middle East. It could end the Plutocratic control of governments here and elsewhere. It could be called "The Energy Revolution".

Uranus in Taurus: March 2019– April 2026; square Saturn in Aquarius December 2021 – December 2022.

The last time Uranus transited Taurus was 1935 through 1942 coinciding with the ongoing Great Depression and the beginning of WW II. Germany invaded and took over Czechoslovakia between September of 1938 and March of 1939. December 7, 1941, the Japanese invaded Pearl Harbor, bringing the U.S. into the war. Economically, the greatest government investment in the economy in our history took place, financing massive troop involvement in Europe and the Far East, and the mobilization of factory workers (mostly women) domestically to build our great war machine. Nobody thought of "budget deficits" in this era. People sacrificed together in a patriotic effort to "save the world". There were coupons issued for everything from gas to butter and few complained about shortages. Concerns about the stock market and capital investment were put aside for the war effort.

Taurus is a sign associated with land, real estate, and the sovereignty of national borders which were breached, invaded and blown up during WW 11. The technological development associated with Uranus was being used for war and developed rapidly with rocketry (the Germans), aviation, and the development of the atomic bomb, later dropped on Japan by the U.S. in 1945.

This transit will more likely correspond with innovative technologies (Uranus) associated with rescuing endangered species, the land, (Taurus), ensuring its continuing fertility, and developing group efforts to bring this about. Enthusiastic and inspired groups of people will likely form eco-villages whose ideas will spread throughout the world, conserving water, soil, heritage seeds, and sustainable architectures. Worker owned businesses, similar to those developed successfully in Argentina (after its economy collapsed in 2002) may gain real traction at this time. The re-localization of economies stressing community life, and people's conscious participation in it will help us get our democracy back as matters are no longer removed and determined by distant Plutocrats and trans-national capitalists.

Ecological Medicine:

In the September 2012 issue of Scientific American, (pp. 78-83), the article "The Great Climate Experiment" is published by Ken Caldeira, a climate scientist from the Carnegie Institution for Science's Department of Global Ecology at Stanford University. He covers probable effects on the atmosphere and life on earth in the near term and the "far future". He states "Compared with the gradual warming of hothouse climates in the past, industrial climate change is occurring in fast-forward. In geologic history, transitions from low- to high-CO_2, atmospheres typically happened at rates of less than 0.00001 degree a year. We are re-creating the world of the dinosaurs 5,000 times faster. What will thrive in this hothouse? Some organisms, such as rats and cockroaches, are invasive generalists, which can take advantage of disrupted environments . . . . .Climate change may usher in a world of weeds."

Taurus is concerned with the land and its ability to sustain life. Out of necessity, we may be rapidly developing "cures" for invasive species and new types of virus, bacteria, and parasites that will be encroaching upon territories further north. Infestations from Asia into the State of Florida such as the snakehead fish and pythons illustrate this point. Mosquitoes, carriers of the great killer, Malaria, are proliferating in more Northern latitudes and carrying new encephalitic viruses. Lyme Disease has been proliferating in the U.S. for the past 40 years as a result of warmer winters that cause a proliferation of deer (carriers of the tick that carries the disease). In Massachusetts, even with spraying, whole communities have been disrupted by the threat of mosquitoes. These invasions are taxing the financial resources of civil societies that are already losing money. Major efforts will be made to inoculate against these diseases. This includes diseases infecting trees and other plant life upon which we have depended for centuries.

Franken-science:

Recently, I attended a lecture in Lexington, Massachusetts given by a scientist who is considered to be one of the world's greatest authorities on what is called "geo-engineering". One of his proposals was delivering massive amounts of sulphuric compounds into the global atmosphere to reflect light back and create a "global cooling". He pointed out that this happens when large volcanoes erupt, spewing this pollution into the atmosphere. A recent example of this was when Mt. Pinatubo erupted in the Philippines in 1994-1996 and lowered the world's mean temperature. When a member of the audience expressed anxiety that this might threaten public health and even kill people, his response was that it may be worth taking this risk to save us from global warming that creates severe droughts and destroys crops. I admit, this scared me!

On October 29th, an article was published in The New York Times called "Geoengineering: Testing the Waters by Naomi Klein. She reports: ". . an American entrepreneur named Russ George dumped 120 tons of iron dust off the hull of a rented fishing boat; the plan was to create an algae bloom that would sequester carbon and thereby combat climate change. Mr. George is one of a growing number of would-be geoengineers who advocate high-risk, large-scale technical interventions that would fundamentally change the oceans and skies in order to reduce the effects of global warming. In addition to Mr. George's scheme to fertilize the ocean with iron, other geoengineering strategies under consideration include pumping sulfate aerosols into the upper atmosphere to imitate the cooling effects of a major volcanic eruption and 'brightening' clouds so they reflect more of the sun's rays back into space. The risks are huge. Ocean fertilization could trigger dead zones and toxic tides. And multiple simulations have predicted that mimicking the effects of a volcano would interfere with monsoons in Asia and Africa, potentially threatening water and food security for billions of people".

We must be vigilant concerning the possibility of a "Franken-science" being implemented in this period either by privately funded billionaires or large government enterprises, making decisions that could balloon out of control and threaten the lives of millions.

The "real" new economy:

As fiat currencies either fail or seriously fluctuate, new ideas about money, barter, and trade will emerge. Financial markets historically tend to "go sideways" during transits of Uranus in Taurus, so less emphasis will be placed on getting rich in the stock market. Old fashioned "barter" markets may reappear. Land ownership and development and farming in a sustainable way will move to the forefront. Since Uranus mobilizes groups, co-housing, eco-villages, group ownership of lands will be considered.

Since Taurus is a sign associated with accounting, there will likely be structural changes to laws and systems governing taxation, new regulations effecting banking, and innovations in the insurance industry. I will elaborate more concerning where I think economies are going in the chapter ahead on Pluto in Capricorn.

The Jupiter/Saturn conjunction in Aquarius in 2020 is square (in conflict) with Uranus in Taurus. This suggests changes in the shape of the nation (Taurus), how it produces electricity (Aquarius), and its governing institutions. Many states will want to "secede" from the U.S. The constitution may change to accommodate the revolutionary fervor, and attempt to keep the nation together by granting more power to states and local governance.

The gap between the rich and the poor will likely continue to widen, increasing instability. Extremes in weather will increase the mass migrations of people to more livable areas. Taurus wishes to "hold on to its territory" and Aquarius wants to share with each other for the "greater good" raising the specter of competing ideologies and solutions. These battles may result in war unless we are able to successfully discuss and debate these issues. If the polarization between political parties and ideologies continue, The U.S. may fall apart, as states threaten to secede from the Union. Progressive, inventive and ecological trends will begin to manifest and bloom into the late 2020s whose changes I will discuss in my last chapter.

Chapter 2

The Challenge to the Financial Power Elites; the Greater Depression, the End of Empire

Pluto in Capricorn (Nov. 28, 2008 – Nov. 20, 2024)
(square Uranus 2012 – 2016)

Previous transits occurred in the 1530s (the Protestant Reformation) and the 1770s (The start of the American Revolution). Pluto was last square Uranus in the last Great Depression of the late 1920s – 1930s

I n Greek/Roman mythology, Pluto was the designated God of Death, the Underworld, and the Afterlife. Thus, in these ancient societies, people were known to have been "making deals" with Pluto so that when they died, they would transit into a pleasant afterlife rather than a punishing one. In the process, Pluto was said to have accumulated great stores of wealth that lay hidden underground in his domain.

Legend has it that Pluto kidnapped Persephone, the beautiful young daughter of Demeter, the goddess of nature, and forced her to be his bride in the underworld. Demeter was so grief stricken and devastated that she covered the world in winter ice, extinguishing life. The other gods found this unacceptable and told Pluto he would have to return Persephone. Being very shrewd, he made a deal with Demeter that she could have her daughter back half of the year if she could return to him, as his wife, in the other half. Consenting to this agreement, Demeter brings about the return of life in the spring and summer and extinguishes it in the fall and winter. The concept of seasonal "death and rebirth" was explained and the first negotiated "custody" settlement was made.

Pluto is enormously powerful. He is the guardian of our own "secret" underworlds, symbolizing our subconscious fear of sexual abuse, subjugation, death and dying, and even where we may wind up afterwards. As a consequence of his "capture" and sexual domination of the young and the beautiful, we make "deals" with him concerning life, death, sexuality, control of wealth and all the deep, dark, primal drives that lie beneath the surface of the human psyche. Will we do anything to get rich, have great sex, retain custody of our offspring? Like Faust, will we make "deals with the devil" to have everything we desire now only to lose our souls to him later on when he comes to claim us? Is Pluto alive and well today? I think so.

Pluto has been transiting the sign of Capricorn since 2008 and will be in this sign until 2024. Historically, astrologers have observed a correlation with stock market crashes, economic recessions and depressions with important planetary transits from late Sagittarius into early Capricorn; like Saturn in 1929, Saturn and Uranus in 1987/88, and the most recent transit of Pluto's direct station at 28 degrees of Sagittarius in September 2008, moving into Capricorn by late November 2008. Pluto is currently square Uranus in Aries until 2016. The last time this took place was during the last Great Depression of the 1930s which was also the last time Uranus transited Aries.

Through the ages, the sign of Capricorn has been broadly associated with privilege, entrenched power, and authority, whether it be the monarchies, royal families, church hierarchies, dictators, or heads of national and international monopoly corporations. It likes to get to the "top" of any organization and remain there, even feeling a strong sense of entitlement to its elite position. Sometimes, these positions have been earned through talent, personal sacrifice, and hard work. Often, the status has been the result of conferred inheritance or having been born into a family of wealth and prominence. The "robber barons" of the early 20th Century fit this category, as did heads of organized crime, and entrenched political party bosses. The term "Plutocrat" originates from our old friend, Pluto, and he is most comfortable in Capricorn where he can hold onto his position.

Legislating Pluto and the Military Industrial Complex:

"The end of democracy and the defeat of the American Revolution will occur when government falls into the hands of the lending institutions and moneyed incorporations." —*Thomas Jefferson*

"Beware the military/industrial complex" — *Dwight Eisenhower*

It is now becoming apparent, since the mid 1970s, that the government in Washington is being "bought out" by the trans-national cartel of giant corporations and banking/financial institutions. Elected officials depend upon big bucks to launch their campaigns. The separation and balance of powers between private enterprise and the government supposedly "by and for the people" has become subverted to mean a government "by and for the corporations".

Since the 1990s, the world of banking and finance has experienced a wave of "deregulation", undoing the 1930s Glass-Steagall law that originally separated conventional lending banking from investment/speculative banking. The so-called Commodity Modernization Act deregulated derivatives trade, the buying and selling of contracts that are "bets" on stocks, commodities, currencies, even the weather. This was once a helpful practice of "hedging" investments and reducing risk, and has now morphed into a global casino. The decision known as "Citizens United" made by the Supreme Court in January 2010, now permits corporations and unions to inundate the media with all the ads they wish for their preferred candidates. This trend has amplified itself into super-PAC infinity, pouring billions of dollars by special interests into political campaigns.

The financial "crash" of 2008 resulted in a massive bailout of banks "too big to fail" under the auspices of two presidents that ran into the trillions of dollars of taxpayer money. Citigroup and Bank of America, the largest financial institutions in 2008 would have failed without government bailouts. AIG, the biggest insurance company in America would have failed without this intervention because they got involved with Goldman Sach's "put" contract (a bet that a market or commodity will go down) on the housing market as the "counterparty".

In an interview in July 2009, on Democracy Now with Amy Goodman, Matt Taibbi, the journalist who writes with great authority on Wall Street in Rolling Stone Magazine, talks about how Goldman Sachs played a key role in the financial bubble and ensuing crash. He states: "Well, in the housing/credit bubble, they played a key role. They may not have played the key role. But they – it's important to remember that the last, the current – that disaster with housing would not have taken place had not investment banks like Goldman Sachs found a way to take bad securities, and sell them off to secondary investors in a process called ' securitization.' Without that process, there would not have been a market for those bad mortgages. And Goldman Sachs, at the height of the boom, was underwriting between seven and eight percent of those non-prime mortgages. So they were a major player in the mortgage market. And what's important to remember about Goldman, in particular, is they were alone on Wall Street in appearing to know that what they were selling was toxic and was bad, because they were betting heavily against this stuff as they were selling it on the market. And they made an enormous profit, whereas Bear and Lehman; thought they had something good, and they ended up being taken down by their own investments."

In 2011, MF Global went down because of a disrupted "call option" on the Euro, wiping out the holdings in their clients' accounts. J.P. Morgan Chase lost billions of their customers' money in a similar transaction. These are all examples of investment banks in the derivatives trade "gaming" the system" and losing big. And this does not even begin to cover the losses in the so-called over-the-counter "dark market", not traded over exchanges. The heads of these giants are getting off the hook in every investigation so far, and the banks themselves are being fined sums that are the rough equivalent of a "slap on the wrist".

Our nation has been descending into a massive black hole of debt for many years, as jobs have fled the country to cheap labor abroad where there are no environmental laws. Thus, most people's taxable income has dropped while the rich have gotten much, much richer. Today's Plutocrats frequently off-shore their income and what remains is taxed at a lower rate since their income is almost all "capital gains", currently taxed at 15%.

Unfortunately, the majority of the American population knew little or nothing about what was going on in the banking and financial system, trusting that their money was "safe" in the hands of their financial managers.

U.S. Plutocrats and "banksters" sold many European nations on the "financialized" sub-prime mortgages and complex derivative contracts, including the infamous "credit default swaps" that passed risk forward into the coffers of these nations on the "financialized" toxic mortgages. Many of these nations have now reached the point of "default". They can no longer support their public infrastructures since the global "crash" of 2008. This has especially affected Greece, Spain, Ireland, Portugal, and Italy. Iceland crashed earlier on and seems to be pulling out on its own. Germany, Norway, Sweden, Denmark, Finland did not participate in the "frenzy" and are considered the best economies in the world at this time. The European Union, led by Germany, has devised bail out packages imposing serious austerity on the troubled nations, attempting to "save" the Union itself and the solvency of the Euro-dollar. In September 2012, the European Central Bank announced that they will buy bonds (as many as it takes) similar to what the U.S. Federal Reserve has been doing, to stave off financial collapse. I am not optimistic that these "solutions" are going to save the European Union. Already, there are riots in the streets of Athens, Greece. The "Occupy" movement is demonstrating in cities throughout Europe. Millions will be reduced to poverty levels not seen in modern times if the Euro collapses. Nations will have to trade in their own individual currencies. The consequences are serious.

Close to Home

Recently, it was reported by the government that 49% of the U.S. population is at or below the "poverty line" that is considered below $40,000 per year for a family of four. The official unemployment rate at the time of this writing at around 8 - 9% is representative only of the people who are currently collecting unemployment. It is estimated that real unemployment of people who are able and want to work, some of whom have given up looking for jobs, is at around 16% to 22%. Thus, we simply have no tax money from the public-at-large to finance the basic infrastructures of our nation; highways, schools, police and fire departments, sewerage and water systems, etc. that are the basic foundation of our civilization. Our great matrix of nonprofit organizations is at risk and the struggling employed Middle Class is inundated with phone calls and mail, begging for donations.

Public pension funds are at risk and, in their present form, are simply unsustainable. A recent Pew research survey found that the gap between state assets and their obligations for public sector retirement benefits is $1.38 trillion. Even NASA, whose pinnacle accomplishments for the U.S. in space is being threatened with severe budget cuts.

According to Governing Data .com, many local governments across the U.S. are filing for bankruptcy. They report: "In June 2012, Stockton, California became the largest U.S. city to file for bankruptcy. San Bernardino, California was the most recent city to approve a bankruptcy filing after City Council members learned the city had only $150,000 left in its bank accounts. Central Falls, R.I and Jefferson County, Ala. Both filed for bankruptcy in 2011. Harrisburg, Pa., and Boise County, Idaho also filed for bankruptcy, but their claims were rejected."

Recently, (August 2012) the famous linguist and political commentator, Professor Emeritus at MIT, Noam Chomsky wrote an article on TomDispatch. com and published on Alternet.org entitled "Do We Have the Makings of a Real Revolution?" He states: "I'm just old enough to remember the Great Depression. After the first few years, by the mid-1930s – although the situation was objectively much harsher than it is today – nevertheless, the spirit was quite different. There was a sense that "we're gonna get out of it," even among unemployed people, including a lot of my relatives, a sense that 'it will get better.' He goes on to say, "It's quite different now. For many people in the United States, there's a pervasive sense of hopelessness, sometimes despair. I think it's quite new in American history. And it has an objective basis."

Military Spending – Money and Lives

Under the current administration in Washington, we have gone from the black hole war in Iraq to the black hole war in Afghanistan, both financing a giant military complex consisting more and more of private contractors, costing trillions of dollars, and adding more and more to our nation's debt. In all fairness, we have left Iraq and there is an attempt, at this writing,

Information current as of Dec. 3, 2012.

to end the war in Afghanistan and reduce military spending.   However, many of the political pundits are blaming senior citizens, children, and the disabled for all this. They are as busy as beavers in Washington devising cuts in Social Security, Medicare and Medicaid, college loans, school aid, food stamps, much of which are the only buffer families have against abject poverty. Millions of both federal and state government jobs have been lost. The poor and the embedded causes of poverty are being virtually ignored.

More alarming still are three recently passed and signed pieces of legislation that I referred to in the previous chapter: the National Defense Authorization Act that makes it legal for the military to capture and detain U.S. citizens without our constitutionally guaranteed right to "due process", the Federal Restricted Buildings and Grounds Improvement Act that severely restricts our constitutional right to peacefully protest (that will effect both the Tea Party and the Occupy Wall Street protest movements), and, finally, the National Defense Resources Preparedness Act that authorizes the president and cabinet officials to take over crucial parts of the U.S. economy not just in national emergencies, but in peacetime.

Big Brother is Watching You (except the banks)

In an article in "Wired.com" on March 15th, author James Bamford reported that the biggest spy center in our nation's history is currently being built in Bluffdale, Utah. He goes on to report: "A project of immense secrecy, it is the final piece on a complex puzzle assembled over the past decade. Its purpose: to intercept, decipher, analyze, and store vast swaths of the world's communications as they zap down from satellites and zip through the underground and undersea cable of international, foreign and domestic networks". He continues: "Flowing through its servers and routers and stored in near-bottomless emails, cell phone calls, and Google searches, as well as all sorts of personal data trails – parking receipts, travel itineraries, bookstore purchases and other digital "pocket litter". I recommend reading the whole article in order that you may grasp just how extensive we have moved into a surveillance state, under military control.

Since the passing of the Patriot Act under Pres. Bush and the Congress, right after the 9/11 attack, the government's right to invade our cell phones, computers, emails, etc. has ballooned. Pres. Obama signed an extension to the Patriot Act increasing the surveillance of U.S. citizens and the power of the government to invade our lives looking for terrorists, but has been amazingly lax in enforcing transparency requirements on the financial transactions of corporate heads and banking giants. The measly 55 member committee recently appointed to investigate the Wall Street derivatives traders who nearly crashed the financial system in 2008 has, so far, at the writing of this book, released almost nothing. However, in September 2012, New York Attorney General Schneideman, indicted JP Morgan Chase in a civil suit for "widespread fraud in the sale of mortgage-backed securities."

Major losses in "casino" derivatives trades gone wrong depleting customers' accounts shut down MF Global and caused losses in the billions at JP Morgan Chase, as stated above. Government investigations have been launched. Recently, Barclays in the U.K., one of the giant transnational banks, was caught manipulating and "gaming" the LIBOR, which is the ongoing interest rate on loans banks use globally. To unravel and expose this could easily crash the whole global banking and financial system since it is likely that about 16 other banks are involved. In addition to all this, many of the "banksters" the government is allegedly investigating and others yet to be discovered are still trading derivatives to the tune of around $700 trillion (according to the Bank of International Settlements), and are still collecting bonuses after collecting taxpayer bailouts. As we can all plainly see, none of these executives in charge of all this are wearing orange jump suits. Throughout the world, billionaires are dominating the marketplace in the practice of "inequality for most". An example is the "richest man in the world", Carlos Slim (as dubbed year after year by Forbes Magazine) who controls the electric grid in Mexico, one of the world's poorest nations.

Interestingly, however, in the U.S., we have over 10% of our citizens currently in prison, the largest percentage of a population of any nation in the world, most of whom are serving sentences related to drug charges many of which are self-inflicted and the largest percentage of whom are poor and from minority groups. In addition, there has been a movement to "privatize" prisons, creating an incentive for police to arrest and imprison more people (often for minor infractions) to make the system more "profitable".

What does the future hold for Pluto?

The last two transits of Pluto in Capricorn coincided with hugely important historic events: the Protestant Reformation in Europe and the formation of the American Revolution. Currently, the scandals that have haunted the Roman Catholic Church in recent years are forcing major reforms within the churches and many more lie ahead.

In America, I see a "Second American Revolution" beginning to form as the Occupy Wall Street protesters gain recognition and organize their movement into a more cohesive political force. By targeting the "One Percent", the OWS people are calling attention to those people who have "bought out" the government, own the mainstream media and have implemented the greatest transfer of wealth from "the people" into their own accounts in history. Currently, their ongoing protests are hardly mentioned in the corporate-controlled mainstream media. Almost no cameras are recording their valiant efforts. They will likely not give up.

Many individual states, out of necessity, will begin to act independently, making their own local laws more powerful and initiating their own reforms, some of which may include local state- run banks. This will reignite the historic conflict between "states rights" and the broader laws of the land. In addition, severe droughts and climate extremes will likely result in food shortages and sky high food prices. This has, throughout history, initiated revolutions and challenges to governments, as illustrated by the French Revolution and, more recently the revolutions in the Middle East, starting in Tunisia when a food vendor set himself on fire in the street protesting food prices and shortages.

From October 2012 through September 2015, Saturn will transit Scorpio, sextile Pluto in December 2012, and will be in Mutual Reception (which means they will cooperate more fully with each other). It will seem as if a plan to stabilize the economy will be considered and put into place. Super Storm Sandy has made us aware how dependent we are upon oil and gas reserves and how vulnerable we are when our electricity goes down. For a while, some parts of the banking economy may appear to hold together, but the underpinnings will be fragile. In the Spring of 2013, the charts of Israel and Iran are activated by the Lunar eclipse in Scorpio conjunct Saturn in

April and the Solar Eclipse in Taurus in May, pointing to a possible war and further instability in the Middle East effecting energy prices.

For a while, the extreme cultural polarizations we have recently witnessed will likely intensify. By April of 2014, the Uranus/Pluto square will collide with the Sun/Saturn square in the chart of the U.S.A. symbolizing a nearly unbearable stalemate between the branches of government, the differing ideologies, the political parties, and the people-at-large. December 2014 and June through September 2015, Saturn crosses President Obama's Midheaven (career point), square his Uranus in a degree associated with crises in the life of presidents. As Neptune transited these degrees in the late 1960s, protests against the Viet Nam war escalated, President Lyndon Johnson announced he would not run again for the office, the Democrats were defeated and President Nixon was elected. Uranus crossed this degree in March of 1981 when there was an attempt on the life of President Reagan. Saturn transiting Scorpio will likely produce such austerity measures in Europe and the U.S. that people will be "taking to the streets". The only "upside" to this may be the above mentioned mutual reception and sextile between Saturn in Scorpio and Pluto in Capricorn opening the door to a long -term solution to the debt crisis, taking us to the "bottom" of this cycle in 2020 when we will begin coming out of the depression.

Currency Crises:

There will likely be major crises with valuation assigned to currencies, including the Euro-dollar and the American dollar. Some European currencies will likely re-localize back into their original form. China is already, with the consent and encouragement of our present government, trading directly in their currency, the yuan, bypassing the dollar and elevating and strengthening their currency into international status. The U.S. dollar has been the global currency since the Breton Woods Conference in 1944. This is changing. As China's currency strengthens and ours weakens, the resulting dollar inflation will help the government pay down its enormous debt but will create havoc with the population-at-large, forcing people to pay much higher prices for goods and services.

Recently, as the LIBOR scandal was exposed, involving Barclays Bank manipulating and gaming global interest rates, an informative interview was published on July 17, 2012 on usawatchdog, an online newsletter. Former Assistant Secretary of the Treasury Paul Craig Roberts (under Pres. Ronald Reagan) was interviewed. He stated that this manipulation has been going on for years in order to keep the entire financial system and big banks from collapse. He surmises that this will result in significant dollar inflation, as the dollar loses its status as world currency.

Suggestions for Real People

All this would lead me to recommend, as I have in the past, that we have holdings in gold (the most ancient form of money), silver, rare earths, income-producing real estate, tillable farm land, and properties located over aquifers. There will be a rush to privatize" local aquifers and water sheds, even though many communities are against this effort as they have found out the corporations are investing little to repair the infrastructures and charge high prices. Commodities, that have been priced lower in the first half of 2012, will likely rise in ensuing years that will be characterized by scarcities, especially farm crops due to climate extremes of drought and/or flooding. However, as people become more impoverished, the demand for products will likely go down (inability to pay), threatening deflation similar to what happened in the 1930s. Therefore, we will have inflation resulting from the government printing money and deflation in some areas resulting from a drop in sales of goods and services. And you thought you were confused before?

According to Forexpros.com (September 3, 2012), graphs on stock market indexes from 2000 to 2012 on the Dow, S&P, and Nasdaq show the "fall" in 2008, a recovery, and a return to about where they were in 2000 showing little growth and change. Graphs on gold starting in 2000 through 2012, show a dramatic and steep rise priced in dollars as shown on shown on Kitco.com. There will likely be the usual historic fluctuations in these markets. However, my take is that the global financial "cartel" and the giant "banksters" will continue to do their best to manipulate these markets, even though they lost control in 2008. All of this would illustrate that the stock market is not friendly to the average investor; only to the "insider initiated". In 2013 – 2014, Saturn's transit in Scorpio would point to a surprising improvement in parts of the economy and some stocks could do well. However, for those privy to the right information, this is a short-term upswing within a longer term cycle in which fundamentals are still dark. The most challenging is the period between 2017 and 2020. Once again, the knowledge "divide" between the 1% and the rest of the nation increases exponentially. In addition, the financial atmosphere promotes derivative trading as opposed to actually buying stocks and making real investments in companies.

On a practical level, I recommend that people move inland (off coastal regions where oceans will be rising) to places of elevation where there is abundant inland fresh water and tillable farmland. It would help to live where there are colleges and universities offering intellectual capital and smart people who are dedicated to devising solutions to our problems. I see a movement developing for cities and towns to encourage small businesses to develop relationships with local universities, exchanging ideas and sharing resources. Changes in long-held ideas and paradigms will take time and will likely start at the smaller, grassroots level.

Suggestions for Emergencies

Recent climate crises have made us aware how unprepared we are when these things hit us locally. Hurricanes Katrina and Sandy are illustrative of this phenomena. Some carefully researched and comprehensive books have been written on how to survive local catastrophes. I would suggest: "How to Survive the End of the World as We Know It: Tactics, Techniques, and Technologies for Uncertain Times" by James Wesley Rawles, SAS Survival Guide for Any Climate, for Any Situation" by John Weisman, and "Emergency Food Storage and Survival Handbook: Everything You Need to Know to Keep Your Family Safe in a Crisis" by Peggy Dianne Layton.

Based on my personal experience, I would recommend storing preserved food with a shelf life of at least 10 years in small individualized meals, potable water, first aid medical supplies, water-proof sleeping bags, blankets, spare clothing packed in plastic bags, flash lights and batteries and medications (if you need them). Pack a bag with your financial records, identifications like your birth certificate and passports, wills and estate records, etc. and have it in a designated place so you can grab it in a hurry. Gas heat and gas fireplaces are good because they do not depend upon electricity to operate. (This is not recommended in heavily earthquake-prone area as gas lines may rupture). A wood-burning stove with a supply of wood is a good option. Keep your car filled with gasoline for a quick escape and avoidance of gas lines. If you are inclined, having a short wave radio system would help. A solar wind-up radio is a really good investment, keeping you in touch with the world when both phone wires and satellite technology go down. There is a great website, beprepared.com that lists and sells "emergency essentials" you can use. Lastly, take a course in first aid as this may save a life.

Competition Abroad

Interestingly, as I stated above, due to the melting of the Eastern Himalayan glaciers, China's rivers are running dry and much of what is left is filled with factory pollution. In order to solve this problem, they are currently buying millions of gallons of fresh water from Canada's Lake Huron. India has also depended upon this glacier melt for thousands of years and will face the ensuing ecological crises that lie ahead. There is a perception among many economists and industrialists that China and India will "rule the world" in the near future. I disagree with this assessment because it will be difficult to survive the loss of water and climate extremes that are developing in these nations. The air pollution in China is so severe that you seldom "see the sky" and people are becoming sick there. Even though China is currently the largest manufacturer of solar panels in the world, the majority of their energy production is still from coal. Factory pollution is extremely heavy since there are no environmental laws to protect the population. As their markets drop in Europe and the U.S., their economy is already softening and will likely worsen in the next few years. They have recently undergone their secretive process of leadership change. With the will to do so, however, China may find some solutions to these issues. Their development in the past 20 years has been nothing short of spectacular. Their conflict with Japan over gas resources in the South China Sea brings the U.S.A. into it as we are pledged to protect Japan and military vessels have already been moved into this area. There is no way that China is going to move away from its policy of getting control of oil and gas resources throughout the world. All economies will be affected by these factors until the 2020s when a new source of energy is tapped.

The return of "the power of the people":

There will be some regions where the people will be reacting violently, hoarding guns, food, water, etc. perceiving that they will have to "defend their turf" as society breaks down. Others will step up to the plate at the grass roots community level to solve economic problems through mutual cooperation. Many of these communities will organize around local organic farming and small entrepreneurial enterprises, a portion of which will be worker owned. Select towns and cities will likely launch combined efforts with neighboring cities toward the common use of utilities, resources, and facilities.

The book "America Beyond Capitalism: Reclaiming our Wealth, Our Liberty, and Our Democracy" by University of Maryland economist Gar Alperovitz outlines a pathway to the "new economy movement" with cooperative banking, worker-owned businesses, and an effective plan for re-localization of the economy with a form of capitalism that is framed democratically. On the August 2, 2012 issue of truthout.org, excerpt from his book, Alperovitz states: "The long trends are ominous: the beginning point of the following study is the painful truth that there is now massive evidence that for decades Americans have been steadily becoming less equal, less free, and less the masters of their own fate....the top 1 percent now garners for itself more income each year than the bottom 100 million Americans combined." It is my belief that we are just beginning to confront these realities and we will ultimately change our direction as we march into the 2020s and into societal and economic transformation.

A return to the Founders

In a sense, there will likely be a "replay" of the American colonies rebelling against the British Empire; but this time, it will be rebelling against an American Empire that Americans no longer want. "Big Brother" watching us will not play well with this nation's citizenry who will likely reclaim its original revolution against the tyranny of both imperial monopoly corporations and "Big Government". The Supreme Court will face a scrutiny it has never before faced on such a wide scale. People will call for them to have accountability with respect to conflicts of interest and extremism, especially since they deemed corporations as having the same rights as persons. They may be seriously challenged as being "the last word" in defining the law of the land.

These monumental conflicts will challenge the powerful both in government and industry, and may bring the U.S. to the edge of bankruptcy. All this may threaten the office of the presidency itself. In 2017, Pluto will oppose the Mars in the astrological chart of the Federal Reserve (December 23, 1913) empowering many who wish to end its existence. The chart of the World Bank (December 27, 1945) and the World Trade Organization (January 1, 1995), all printed in the back of this book are being hit heavily by Pluto. They will either collapse or be drastically reorganized in this cycle. I would call this the "disestablishment of the establishment". An excellent article was published in the Spring/Summer Edition of The NCGR Geocosmic Journal; "Cycles of Uranus, Pluto, and Hades, by Joyce Levine highlighting the history behind aspects of Pluto to Uranus and the serious difficulties and challenges that lie ahead.

The Saturn/Pluto square of 1993 coincided with the signing of "NAFTA", the decline of the Japanese economy, the beginning of the deregulation of the banks and trans-national corporations, the public going onto the internet, and the rise of China into the world's second largest economy. Saturn in Capricorn conjunct Pluto in January of 2020 will likely signify the "bottom" of this Great Depression and a will to eliminate the institutions and trade agreements that have served only elite groups. This will likely transform the fundamentals of global trade and the monopoly economy. In December of 2020, Jupiter will be conjunct Saturn in Aquarius, ushering in a new era in technology, global politics, and economic paradigms that will begin to rise in earnest when Pluto goes into Aquarius in January of 2024.

Surviving the decline – darkness into light

AlterNet posted an article on May 7, 2012 (TomDispatch.com); "Surviving America's Decline" by Ernest Callenbach, the author of "Ecotopia" a seminal work on a future world in which humans live in concert with life on earth and in harmony with one another. This document was found on the author's computer after his recent death. Seeing the turmoil that lies ahead, he felt moved, as he knew he was dying, to share his ideas about how to survive these times. He outlined and elaborated on hope, mutual support, practical skills, to organize, to learn to live with contradictions. His disappointment is palpable as he had great hopes for America and the world-at-large to step up and address what is necessary for the greater good. He wrote: "So I look to a long-term process of 'succession', as the biological concept has it, where 'disturbances' kill off an ecosystem, but little by little new plants colonize the devastated area, prepare the soil for larger and more complex plants (and the other beings who depend on them), and finally the process achieves a flourishing, resilient, complex state – not necessarily what was there before, but durable and richly productive. In a similar way, experiments under way now, all over the world, are exploring how sustainability can in fact be achieved locally. Technologically, socially, economically – since it is quite true, as ecologists know, that everything is connected to everything else, and you can never just do one thing by itself."

A co-founder of the successful EcoVillage at Ithaca, New York, author Liz Walker has shared her extensive knowledge about creating a new and sustainable way of life in her book: "Choosing a Sustainable Future". This book contains a treasure of information about organic farming, local business, local democracy and community cooperation, all born out of her actual experiences. EcoVillage has formed partnerships with Cornell University in the green movement, renewable energy, and new technologies to solve the problems that lie before us. She writes: "I believe we have an extra moral obligation to turn around our way of life, to learn 'to live simply that others may simply live.' But rather than just feeling guilty or overwhelmed by these multiple crises (which we all feel at times), we may also be lucky enough to recognize something else – we do have a choice to learn to live differently, as individuals, as communities and as a culture. There is a wonderful upwelling of energy to make profound changes that are not only necessary, but that also lead to a much higher quality of life."

For my own part, as long as there are people, like this, whose lives are inspired and dedicated to that which lies beyond the self-absorbed, insensitive controllers who seem to dominate today's discourse, I hold out hope. I hold out hope for my grandchildren and all other children whose resilience, creativity, and determination have not been snuffed out yet. I hold hope in my heart as the sun shines on new life at the dawn of each day and rests peacefully as the constellations emerge at night to tell their story. The story is: this will all change. The "gods" will return to earth, reborn anew out of the souls of each and every one of us.

Chapter 3

The Consequences of Global Climate Change, the Great Melt, Mass Extinctions, the Return of the Great Spirit

Neptune in Pisces

February 4, 2012 – March 30, 2025

Previous periods of this transit: 1520 – 1534, 1685 – 1699, 1848 – 1863, 2011 – 2026.

(Entered April 4, 2011 – Aug. 4th 2011, enters Feb. 3rd 2012 – March 30th 2025, enters retrograde Oct. 22nd 2015 through Jan. 26th 2026.

The lengthy transit of Neptune in its own "home base" sign of Pisces is a subject so vast in its scope that it is worthy of a book all its own. There is an excellent essay published in the December/January (2012) issue of The Mountain Astrologer, by Michele Finey entitled "Into the Blue: Neptune in Pisces" that makes excellent reading on this subject that by its very nature is challenging to comprehend.

Neptune's expression in Greco/Roman mythology is as the ancient and powerful god of the sea. When angered, Neptune could summon tsunamis, hurricanes, and storms seemingly out of nowhere, sinking ships, changing the course of battles at sea. He could create mists and fogs that obscure the line of sight and wreck seafarers on the rocks and shoals. His symbol is the "trident", an instrument that acted like a magic wand that could create a storm or clear the air, magically forming a wonderful ambiance that any sailor knows and appreciates.

Neptune was actually discovered in 1846 at a time when it was conjunct Saturn and in the sign it has recently left, Aquarius. Since Neptune is known for its rulership of oceans, fluids, chemicals, it is interesting it was discovered when the planet Saturn, symbolizing structure and definition, lent it a framework. Famous for being nebulous, confusing, intoxicating and uplifting, Neptune is a planet of expanded consciousness beyond ordinary perceptions. It is the "stuff of dreams". It often erodes previous structures and boundaries, whether in politics, religion, or science and is capable of opening up passages to great truths or permission for great deceptions, cures for diseases or snake oil, anesthesia or addictive substances. So goes the symbol for Pisces; two fish swimming in opposite directions. Interestingly, this is the ancient inscription associated with the beginning of Christianity at the dawn of the Piscean Age, over 2000 years ago.

In the 1500s, Neptune's transit through Pisces saw the spread of the Protestant Reformation, (a backlash to extreme corruption in the Roman Catholic Church). It corresponded with an outbreak of the Plague, during which time the great seer and physician, Nostradamus, stopped the outbreak in various cities by burning corpses and cleaning up the streets. In 1522, Magellan circumvented the globe, inspiring world trade, which led to the collapse of the Aztec, Inca and Toltec civilizations instigated by Spanish invaders, mostly because of the diseases they spread. In 1692, the famous Salem witch trials took place in a frenzy of religious fanaticism among the Puritan colonists who, ironically, had traversed the ocean to have the freedom to practice their religion in the New World.

In 1858, the famous Bernadette of Lourdes claimed to have seen visions of the Blessed Virgin and discovered a natural spring there, whose waters are thought to this day to have miraculous healing powers. The California "gold rush" moved thousands of people to endure immeasurable hardships to travel by wagon train and on horseback into the western United States, searching for their "dream".

In August of 1859, oil was discovered in Titusville, Pennsylvania fueling the industrial revolution, leading to a unprecedented prosperity and raising of living standards for billions of people. It also framed our current modern civilization's dependency on oil for the vast amounts of energy we now use. Now, we are confronted with the resulting polluting of our land and waters, global climate extremes, and the challenge to the continuance of fossil fuel energy usage that we face today.

During this period, Karl Marx published his "Communist Manifesto" and Charles Darwin published his "Origin of Species", both challenging political, economic, and scientific assumptions of their time. In the U.S., the abolitionist movement organized itself which later led to the Civil War and the end to the institution of slavery. Florence Nightingale established the profession of nursing, the microscope was developed, and Lister and Pasteur and their colleagues discovered micro-organisms as a source of disease. Breakthroughs were made with the development of vaccines, anesthetics, cleanliness and hygiene. In a sense, this time frame formed the gateway to modern medicine.

What Now?

Based on the aspects and how they have played out historically, my interpretation of what lies ahead involves the manifestation of a multitude of planetary crises around the availability of fresh water. The increased heat in many locations throughout the world will threaten desertification and loss of potable water. In other areas, monsoon type rains may cause extreme flooding. There is already an acceleration of the rate of glaciers melting and inundation of coastal regions. Many of these disappearing glaciers are in mountain ranges upon which huge populations have depended for fresh water for thousands of years such as India, China, and the western United States, as I discussed in previous chapters. Due to flooding, many island nations may no longer exist within a relatively short time period and many native cultures will be forced to leave their habitats. We have been reminded recently of the consequences of great hurricanes such as Hurricane Katrina and Super Storm Sandy.

The April 13, 2012 "Common Dreams.org" released reports by United Press International entitled "Historic sea level rise in Pacific studied". It stated "Sea levels in the Southwest Pacific have risen dramatically since the late 19th century, a study by Australian and British researchers shows. Scientists at the University of Queensland, with colleagues in British universities said sea levels in Tasmania remained relatively stable for much of the past 6,000 years but around 1880 they started rising dramatically, increasing almost 8 inches in the last century."

Tsunamis like the catastrophe in 2004 in Indonesia and the 2011 disaster in Japan will likely increase. Many of these have nothing to do with the activities of our civilization. However, we will have to confront the possibility that deep sea drilling for oil not only produces disasters like the BP oil eruption in the U.S. in 2010, but may disturb fissures in the earth under the sea and contribute to tectonic instability.

Out of great necessity, there will be movements that have already started for economic equal opportunity and a "dethroning" of the handful of people who control most of the world's money and resources. An intense focus will be on re-localizing economies;, i.e. raising food, conserving and recycling water, and community efforts toward survival rather than depending upon national and trans-national institutions.

There will likely be breakthroughs in medicine and cures for major diseases that currently afflict us, many of which will rise out of discoveries in genetic research and engineering. However, we will have to spend our already exhausted capital on cleaning up the vast pollution in oceans and waterways in which the ancient chains of life support have been threatened. Some nations may be so desperate, they may be drilling for deep underground aquifers in desert regions where supplies have been exhausted. Tropical diseases may move further north as the globe continues to heat up, increasing the pace of development for finding cures to diseases like malaria that have haunted us for thousands of years.

During Neptune's last transit, the California "gold rush" captured the attention of America, as thousands migrated west to make a fortune. Most died on the way or spent the rest of their lives searching for the great gold strike that eluded them. Only a very few found and were able to acquire the gold mines producing the fortunes they dreamed about. In these times, gold may, once again, be acquired and hoarded as a result of wide-spread poverty and a lack of confidence in the stability of currencies.

We are currently experiencing mass extinctions of species not known since the dinosaurs went down. In order to save ourselves, we will likely be forced to develop and implement new non-fossil fuel forms of energy. As stated in previous chapters, I am of the opinion that breakthroughs will be made in answer to this need. The last time Pluto was square Uranus was the 1930s when the massive drought in the U.S. resulted in the "Dust Bowl", the greatest environmental disaster in our history. The record droughts in the U.S. in 2012 evoked memories of that catastrophe. Earthquakes and volcanic activity are likely to increase in number during this period. Neptune rules liquids, from oil, to water to molten magma movements underground.

Food for the soul:

Our society will have to come face to face with the fact that turning to drugs, both legal and illegal is alarmingly popular and wide spread. There is already a great debate about why we are losing the "war on illegal drugs". In addition, we will likely have to admit to ourselves that huge pharmaceutical corporations are generating equally huge profits by legally selling drugs that temporarily alleviate symptoms but do not deal at all with core problems. For far too many people, they foster addictions and dependencies that threaten human health in general. There are already extensive controversies concerning the legalizing of marijuana as some states have recently passed laws allowing the sale and use of "medical marijuana". In addition, many drugs used to treat depression, insomnia, and anxiety are being "called into question" as they tend to eventually "not work" and create even more serious health problems when used over large periods of time.

All these now seemingly inescapable problems may bring about a realization that this tragic trend is symptomatic of a society in great pain and despair; devoid of nourishment for its soul, a subject of grave concern for spiritual Neptune. In modern times, few people have escaped the singular trap consisting of a core belief only in a world of "mechanistic materialism"; that you have to be dead to be scientifically "verifiable"; that you have to be ruthlessly materially competitive to survive. This brings with it a terrible consequence; an ensuing loss of a sense of beauty, compassion, and an uplifting sense of spiritual presence. We may have to face that many people turn to drugs because they are living lives without real meaning, a sense of higher purpose, or concern for the "greater good". Other groups of people, feeling overwhelmed and confused, may turn to religious fanaticism; further partitioning themselves into being "right" and condemning others to being "wrong". Wars have been fought over these issues. They still are.

In modern times, Neptune is the "ruler" of the marketing and advertising industry and is a master at "programming" the masses to buy products, elect candidates, and then "go back to sleep". We are "Neptuned" on a daily basis by television ads, internet ads, radio ads, magazine ads, etc. One of the founders of modern psychology, Sigmund Freud, pointed out the many dark "subconscious" drives that motivate people beneath our so-called civilized surface, and this information (largely Plutonian) is cleverly used by the huckster Neptunians to sell us anything and everything, including the promise of "eternal pleasure". These times could very well motivate us to "wake up" and make the decision to be aware of our complicity in our own self-deception.

The best of Neptune:

Neptune and Pisces are all about meaning and purpose, kindness and understanding, openness to discovery, and a sense of "oneness" with the earth and each other. Albert Einstein, a Pisces, said, "Either nothing is a miracle or everything is a miracle", framing the dilemmas of our times. Water, Neptune's element, is the source of all life as we know it, but it is just as capable of drowning life in great floods, storms and tsunamis. A yearning for spiritual understanding can be overwhelming or invigorating. Inherent within Neptune's grand contradictions resides our power to choose: escapism or confrontation, lies or truths, fanaticism or spiritual realization, death or life.

Neptune also is the composer and performer of music; sounds and rhythms that elevate us, move us, inspire us. In its own sign of Pisces, the resonate frequency of the earth and its oceans may be changing. A new music may be composed and played around the world, uniting and embracing humanity within the sphere of its magnificent sounds.

The Hopi Indians have a tradition that these are the times when humanity will choose either to destroy itself or will take a higher pathway and join with the Great Spirit to bring about a new and harmonious human presence on the earth. The Hindu tradition speaks of the return of the god, Krishna, who will take humanity to a higher more spiritual version of itself. Scientific discoveries may propel us beyond what we know as time and space into a true realization of our presence in a multi-dimensional reality. We may even experience a grand metamorphosis from being a "creature" to being a creature -creator. Spirituality and science may no longer be competitors, but instead recognize that one is the "supreme intelligence" of the force of creation itself and the other studies and examines what has been created.

I am of the opinion that "The Great Spirit" has been here all along. It awaits our recognition; blind eyes that will see, minds that will awaken, lost hearts that will beat once more. Neptune's message is one of universal unconditional love that will bind us together into eternity.

Chapter 4

The Aquarian Age.
What Survives Will Rise

Pluto in Aquarius

(Sextile Neptune in Aries and Trine Uranus in Gemini)

January 22, 2024 – March 9, 2043

(Pluto last transited in Aquarius 1778 – 1798)

The sign of Aquarius, The Water Bearer, is traditionally "ruled" by what I call the "wow" planet Uranus. As I mentioned earlier, Uranus was discovered in the truly impressive period during which Pluto previously transited Aquarius. These times produced the American Revolution (war fought and won), the French Revolution, and the Industrial Revolution. In terms of the trajectory of accomplishments in human history, this is truly impressive. It also describes the Age of Enlightenment that produced the founding fathers of America, who were inspired by the ideals of Democracy, the rule of law, human rights, science and invention, and equality of opportunity.

This is in sharp contrast with the sign in which Pluto is transiting now, where a few trans-national capitalists virtually control the world. Ironically, this is exactly the atmosphere that gave birth to the American and French revolutions; i.e., bad decisions and unfair taxation by the monarchs during ecological crises and famines. There was resentment by the colonists of the dominance of Royal monopolies that controlled commerce and economies back then, along with taxes imposed upon them by the monarchy. You may remember the Boston Tea Party rebellion and the cry "Taxation without representation!"

In a way, this is "de-ja-vu all over again", but, this time, involving much of the world-at-large as we struggle against powerful forces to reclaim our rights to "life, liberty, and the pursuit of happiness". Then, information went out via Tom Paine and Ben Franklin's press or by word-of-mouth. Today, opinions can "go viral" on the internet.

In these times, there is a sense of urgency concerning the survival of humankind as we come face to face with the fact that our "success" at creating the highest standard of living the world has ever known may be at the expense of life on earth. In other words, the ancient notion of "apocalypse" brought upon us by a deity or a force of nature, may, instead be brought about by our own greed, selfishness, short-sightedness, and, most of all, indifference to the evidence before us.

Many people with whom I have had these conversations over the past few years are of the opinion that this is "human nature" and it will likely never change. I will state, out front, that I disagree. I think human beings have a "nature" that we have barely touched. The miraculous history of life on earth has produced a massive tide of the evolution of species and thereby intelligence that has taken us to amazing heights; from the few who survived the Ice Age to the many who now live in the Space Age.

The looming issue today may be that our technological innovation has surpassed our psychological and spiritual development. We are adolescents, stuffing ourselves with fast food, buying products by the millions that are filling landfills to stupefying levels, and playing with nuclear weapons. Our own children have grown up with violent movies, violent computer games, violent television, and now, an increasingly violent society. All of this has been about appealing to the lowest and most compulsive level of the human psyche in order to sell millions of products to make a handful of people rich. Our society is so polarized that our political process in Washington is frequently paralyzed, and hate-mongering abounds in campaigns, on television, and on internet sites. So, here we are. The choice is simple. We have to either grow up or go down.

Growing up into a Super Humanity:

In the September 2012 special issue of Scientific American, Robert M. Sapolsky, Professor of biology and neurology at Stanford University, wrote an article entitled "Super Humanity" (pp. 40 to 43). He states: "The fact that we have created and are thriving in this unrecognizable world proves a point – namely, that it is in our nature to be unconstrained by our nature. We are no strangers to going out of bounds. Science is one of the strangest, newest domains where we challenge our hominid limits. Some of the most dramatic ways in which our world has been transformed are the direct products of science, and the challenges there are obvious. Just consider those proto-geneticists who managed to domesticate some plants and animals – an invention that brought revolutionary gains in food but that now threatens to strip the planet of its natural resources."

In this spirit, our technological development is staggering. Robots at work beneath the sea and on Mars, engineered stem cells, an international space station, vehicles that can transport us anywhere on earth, computer chips that mimic the flexible arrangement of neurons in animal brains, internet technology and hand held devices that develop so fast that yesterday's equipment is quickly obsolete. We are already marching toward being "androids" as limbs are being replaced, organs are being "regenerated" and theories about rewiring our brains are being debated. There is a lot of science fiction out there that hypothesizes humans replacing themselves with robots, discussion about biological life vs. intelligent machines, etc.

The End of Empire:

As the last transit of Pluto in Aquarius initiated the long decline of monarchies, this transit will likely reflect the end of empires and so-called "super powers". The ideal of "Democracy" will be recycled and renewed and it will be recognized that it is not effective when it gets too big. Democratic governance works well when it is more localized and comprehensible; less subject to mass imaging and more subject to accountability. The vast and growing contents of the internet will enable us to access information around the globe, but it is local education that teaches us discrimination and critical thinking. Loving and concerned parents and real, live, caring teachers being present fully in the lives of young people is what gets the job done. Herein resides the hope for a better future.

A New and Different America:

The 2020s through the 2040s will likely see the end of America as we currently know it. Either many of the states will secede from the Union or the Union will become a loose confederation of states, closer to where it was originally. Local governments will likely be stronger than the central government in Washington. We will have to figure out the big projects for our betterment that can be done by the government in Washington v. the more localized projects better done within states and communities. This has been a long struggle in our history and we now have the chance to "get it right". The ideal of equality of opportunity will be strong, the economy will be better, technology will be spectacular. However, cultural differences will still divide our nation, as they will in the nations of Europe. In Asia, many economies will improve, but they will likely be ethnically divided as well. People will be struggling to adapt new technologies to nations whose water supplies and access to food will be seriously threatened. Many low-lying coastal regions and island nations will be disappearing due to rising oceans. The boundaries and geography of nations will be changing dramatically. Mass immigrations of people to areas that can support human population will escalate.

E. Alan Meece, in his book, "Horoscope for the New Millennium" (p 285) writes: "Not only will Pluto be making its karmic return in America's chart in the 2020s, so will Uranus – and Neptune will be opposing its natal position. This indicates that a great American crisis, another 'hinge of history' comparable to the Revolution, the Civil War, and World War II, is due in the middle 2020s. The United States will pursue another 'struggle for its very existence.'"

On December 14, 2020, a total solar eclipse occurs, just one week before the Jupiter/Saturn conjunction in Aquarius, the first of its kind in over 700 years. The solar eclipse of April 8, 2024 shows Jupiter and Uranus on the Midheaven in Washington, D.C. These herald dramatic changes and movements toward possible war, rebellion, and threats to the cohesiveness of the nation.

January 26, 2026, Neptune enters Aries. As it later moves into a sextile with Pluto and Uranus (when it goes into Gemini), I have great hopes for the emergence of the authentic Aquarian Age. Although old remnants of previous human drives and motivations will linger, I believe a grand consciousness change will elevate the human spirit. The notion will prevail that we need to band together to implement solutions, creating new and prosperous economies, and, most of all, that we are being compelled to learn how to live sustainably and cooperatively. Aquarius is a sign associated with tolerance, friendship, and group cooperation. This will help us get through the cultural polarizing elements that have been asserting themselves today.

Traveling to other planets and sending probes to other solar systems will become highly probable as nations will embark upon joint enterprises in the development of energy and in space. Scientific discoveries defy national borders and will benefit us all as we break through barriers of "tribal" consciousness into a clearer sense that we are all inhabitants and travelers together on planet earth. Medical science will advance and target research on the brain and nervous system which may enhance intelligence, cure mental illnesses including dementia and depression. It was recently announced that a treatment for depression, Transcranial Magnetic Stimulation (TMS), the device being called Neurostar and manufactured by Neuronetics has been approved by the FDA. This may be the beginning of a new branch of medicine we might call "energy healing" that may very well advance in the Aquarian cycle.

The Horoscope for the New Millennium: (January 1, 2000, 12:00 AM EST, Washington, D.C.)

The book, Horoscope for the New Millennium, by E. Alan Meece is an amazing and comprehensive look at the serious challenges and grand opportunities that may lie ahead for humanity. He writes: "The Chart for the New Millennium may also hold clues about how each individual can cross over 'The Mountain' into the 'Promised Land'."

It is at this point that I turn to this horoscope since the "progressions" in this chart point to times of serious significance and marked change. The first one, we have discussed earlier (2008 – 2011) coincided with the onset of a great depression. Mercury is square Mars in 2020, confirming a danger of wars and conflict in America and Europe. The transiting Jupiter/Saturn conjunction in December 2020 also marks the end of this great depression cycle. Mercury is conjunct Uranus in 2022 showing grand technological breakthroughs in energy and, unfortunately, weaponry. As Neptune enters Aries (last in this sign during the Civil War), Uranus goes into Gemini (last in this sign during WWII), Jupiter and Saturn both turn direct in 2024-2025, marking a second crisis in the Millennium chart. Civil war could break out in the U.S.A., which is the worst case scenario. A viable alternative could be that the Union stays together with increasing decentralization and more power given over to individual states. We will have to confront our historic past; enslavement of Africans and genocides of native Americans, along with all our struggles with immigration, racism, and military dominance. I believe, however, that many emergent grass roots movements will have inspired intrinsic changes in the way we live with nature and with one another, potentially putting an end to the dominance of these ancient evils.

The Mars square Neptune in this chart that also contains a Moon in Pisces, again warning us of a lingering but monumental struggle over oil and emergencies pertaining to water resources. This struggle will likely enhance our motivation to invent our way out of these crises. We will likely be concentrating on local economies, energy production, and environments, but connected through internet and satellite technologies to the world. The challenge will to be conscious of both the "up close and personal" and the open minded and international. We need to concentrate on effective local management of our environment and economies and yet have respect and strong connections with nations around the world. This will be more probable when we no longer are fighting over fossil fuel reserves.

My take, as I have stated in previous chapters, is that nuclear fusion and an array of new energy technologies will be discovered and infrastructures will be built, as Pluto, Uranus, and Neptune trine and sextile one another. The Space Age will more fully mature as nations come together in joint efforts to explore other planets and set up stations on the Moon and Mars, probes placed on asteroids, and, just maybe, we may be in contact with intelligent forms of life on other planets.

It is obvious that the many choices and decisions we make along the way will determine whether we deteriorate or evolve, fall apart or rebuild, destroy ourselves or save ourselves.

An Advanced Species:

The great pattern in the heavens consisting of Pluto in Aquarius, Neptune in Aries, and Uranus in Gemini, all in harmonious relationship to one another, is so exciting in its potential that it lends inspiration to the power of human possibility. Within this constellational pattern, humanity may have support from "the universe" to advance to new technological heights, cures for illnesses, and new social and economic paradigms that produce an array of opportunities. .

An historical and monumental opportunity may emerge from all these vast and challenging landscapes. We may actually make a "leap" as a species to a level of scientific development and spiritual understanding never achieved before. In the epic book and film: "2001, A Space Odyssey", science fiction author Arthur C. Clarke presents a "monolith", a tall dark structure that appeared when humans evolved from apes into humans. Later in the story, after a grand struggle between an astronaut and the computer who controls the space vehicle he is in, the monolith appears again as the old human dies and is released into space as a new embryo. I have long felt that this work contained a special prophecy. First, we must we master our own enchantments with our inventions and cease to "worship them as the "golden calf" as portrayed in the epic story of Moses. The worship of "mechanistic materialism" places a severe limitation on the human experience and denies the very existence of the innate creativity and expansive possibility that life presents.

Once this has been conquered, a new extension of our own species may rise to encompass a mastery of time and space as never before. This new form of human expression may reach way beyond the "predator-prey" concept of life on earth into a universal expression of cooperation, wisdom, and understanding spoken of only by the great avatars and prophets of history. Some think this vision will take a miracle to become a reality.

Recently a message from astronaut Dr. Edgar Mitchell was published celebrating the 40th birthday of the Institute of Noetic Sciences of whom he is a founding member. He writes:

"When I went to the moon, I was a pragmatic test pilot, engineer, and scientist. My experience had shown beyond all question that science works. But there was another aspect to my experience during Apollo 14, and it contradicted the 'pragmatic engineer' attitude. It began with the breath-taking experience of seeing planet Earth floating in the vastness of space.

The presence of divinity became almost palpable, and I knew that life in the universe was not just an accident based on random processes. This knowledge came to me directly—noetically. Clearly, the universe had meaning and direction. Then my thoughts turned to daily life on the planet. With that, my sense of wonderment gradually turned into something close to anguish.

It seemed as though humans were unconscious of their individual role in – and individual responsibility for – the future of life on the planet. Science, for all its technological feats, had a limited worldview.

When we see our fundamental unity with the processes of nature and the functioning of the universe – as I so vividly saw it from the Apollo spacecraft – the old ways of thinking and behaving will disappear.

Throughout history people have sought to resolve the differences between their objective methods and their subjective experience – between outer and inner. Humanity needs to rise from the personal to the transpersonal; from self-consciousness to cosmic consciousness.. .

This union of head and heart, insight and instinct, will ensure that as science comes to comprehend the nonmaterial aspect of reality as well as it knows the material, our knowledge will become wisdom, our love of power will become the power of love, and the universal aspect of cosmic consciousness can then emerge."

As we observe the constellations in our universe unfold, and their story is told through multifaceted voices and dimensions of human history, I see that all our endings are just beginnings; that each person alive today is part of this plan. When we step into it and do our part, it begins to come together in a larger sense. Whether your passion is medicine or music, oceanography or architecture, nurturing parent or astronaut; it is all part of a magical unfolding of the potential of all life on this planet. Still, the choice is ours. There are no unimportant lives lived here.

Welcome to the Aquarian Age!

Index to Planets and Signs Pertaining to Historic Cycles in Human History

Aries – Cardinal Fire, Ruling Planet – Mars

Pioneers, aspires, energizes, invents, rebels to insure the rights of the individual. An Aries cycle begins everything anew after the destruction of the old systems. It represents war and armaments or new inventions; social rebellions or the introduction of new societal concepts.

Taurus – Fixed Earth, Ruling Planet – Venus

Builds, constructs, secures, finances, owns. A Taurus cycle secures ownership of real estate either through conquest or purchase, decides national boundaries, repairs infrastructure through civil engineering or building construction, and determines the distribution of wealth.

Gemini – Mutable Air, Ruling Planet – Mercury

Grasps and communicates ideas, develops language skills and locomotion, educates children and socially interacts with relatives and neighbors. A Gemini cycle emphasizes mass educational projects, new modes of travel, the press, clever inventions, and competition (sibling rivalry) for attention.

Cancer – Cardinal Water, Ruling Planet (satellite) – The Moon

Develops feeling and intuition to ensure comfort and survival, is concerned with food and medicine, nurtures and feeds the young, secures fundamental cultural values in families and nations. A Cancerian cycle reveres history and tradition, is patriotic, nationalistic, and frequently retreats into defending the nation against outsiders.

Leo – Fixed Fire, Ruling Planet (star) The Sun

Promotes dramatic self-expression, creativity and entrepreneurship, reveres children, supports leadership skills, sports, and the media arts. A Leo cycle challenges leaders in governments and industries to rise or fall based on their charisma, showmanship, and their ability to inspire others. The dangers that are present lie in movements toward dictatorship.

Virgo – Mutable Earth, Ruling Planet – Mercury

Is concerned with perfecting skills in the job market, the rights of workers, health and human services, and the military service. A Virgo cycle frequently reflects difficulties and challenges related to employment or unemployment and the need for corporate efficiency and productivity. Sanitation, Hygiene, and civil improvements in the quality of life are major concerns.

Libra – Cardinal Air, Ruling Planet – Venus

Creates balance and diplomacy among individuals and nations, works toward equality of opportunity for all, and negotiates peace agreements. A Libra cycle attempts to settle disputes and stop wars and is therefore often accused of indecision and slowing up of the process. This cycle is usually led by idealists and is famous for peaceful protest movements.

Scorpio – Fixed Water, Ruling Planet – Pluto (co-ruled by Mars)

Intensifies, concentrates, and confronts the crises born of the use and misuse of power. It rules over volcanoes and earth changes, and nuclear confrontations when combined with planetary tensions. A Scorpio cycle often decides who controls the collective financial resources of a nation and whether it is used for destructive or constructive purposes, thereby bringing about explosive confrontation among various contenders for this control.

Sagittarius – Mutable Fire, ruling Planet – Jupiter

Expands economies and civilizations throughout the glob e, through travel, trade, and information technologies. A Sagittarius cycle is one of unbridled optimism, continuing to borrow, speculate, and explore until it simply runs out of funds or has consumed all its resources. It will resort to war in order to continue it expansionary efforts and eventually exhausts the treasury bringing the cycle to a halt.

Capricorn – Cardinal Earth, ruling Planet – Saturn

Contracts, limits, and defines national policies, often corresponding with economic recessions or depressions, and forces a "changing of the guard" in both economic and state governance. Frequently, the old power structures fail and fall, giving new people a chance to step up to the plate and take on the heavy responsibilities of devising an entirely new order, with a vision that extends over the long term.

Aquarius – Fixed Air, ruling Planet – Uranus

Invents, transforms and organizes groups to participate in technological breakthroughs, social experiments, and new ideas. Aquarius is the sign behind the concept of democracy, liberty, freedom and intellectual enlightenment. It is associated with the discovery and harnessing electricity. This cycle usually brings forth scientific discoveries that effect the masses of people for generations to come.

Pisces – Mutable Water, Ruling Planet – Neptune (co-ruler Jupiter)

Dissolves previously held convictions and beliefs about life, yearns for a journey to other worlds and states of consciousness through travel over the ocean to new adventures or "trips" that result from the use of substances such as drugs or alcohol. It symbolizes liquids, thus bringing up issues over water (drought or flooding), oil and chemicals. A Pisces cycle can produce geniuses or religious fanatics, great artists, musicians and film-makers or suicidal drug addicts. More than anything, this cycle seeks to express what lends a greater meaning to life beyond ordinary existence.

Bibliography

"Chronicle of the 20th Century" conceived and published by Jacque Legrand, Editor in Chief, and Clifton Daniel.

Mail Online, September 9, 2011, "Britain has joined forces with America"

Scientific American, June 2012 Issue, "Fusion's Missing Pieces" by Goeff Brumfiel

Wall Street Journal, Jan. 27, 2012, "No Need to Panic About Global Warming" (signed by 16 scientists) and Wall Street Journal Feb. 1, 2012 "Response (signed by 39 scientists)

The New York Times, October 29, 2012 Issue, "Geoengineering: Testing the Waters" by Naomi Klein

"Fuel on the Fire: Oil and Politics in Occupied Iraq"by Greg Muttil; Interview on TomDispatch.com, August 27, 2012.

Common Dreams.org, March 31, 2012, "Neurotoxic Pesticides"

Scientific American, September 2012 Issue, "The Great Climate Experiement" by Ken Caldeirc

TomDispatch.com and Alternet.org, "Do We Have the Makings of a Real Revolution" by Noam Chomsky

Wired.com" March 15, 2012, "Biggest Spy Center in our Nation's History" by James Banford

Usawatchdog.com, " Interview with Paul Craig Roberts"

http://earthquake.usgs.gov/earthquakes/map

www.governingdata.com

www.forexpros.com

www.kitco.com

"America Beyond Capitalism: Reclaiming Our Wealth, Our Liberty, and Our Democracy", 2005, by Gar Alperovitz, Wiley Publishers

The NCGR Geocosmic Journal, Spring/Summer Edition, "Cycles of Uranus, Pluto and Hades" by Joyce Levine

Information Clearing House: "Matt Taibbi Probes Role of Investment Giant in US Financial Meltdown" by Democracy Now, July 15, 2009

Common Dreams.org "American Dream Has Become a Myth" Interview published in Der Spiegel of Joseph Stiglitz

AlterNet.com, May 7, 2012, "Surviving America's Decline" by Ernest Callenbach

"Choosing a Sustainable Future" by Liz Walker, 2010, New Society Publishers

The Mountain Astrologer, December/January 2012 Issue, "Into the Blue: Neptune in Pisces" by Michele Finey

Common Dreams.org, April 13, 2012 release from United Press International, "Historic sea level rise in Pacific studied"

Scientific American, September 2012 Issue, "Super Humanity" by Robert M. Sapolsky

"Horoscope for the New Millennium", by E. Alan Meese, 1997 Llewellyn Publications

"The Book of World Horoscopes" by Nicholas Campion, Second Edition published 1995 by Cinnabar Books

Institute of Noetic Sciences membership@noetic.org, September 21, 2012; Message from

Edgar Mitchell

LINDA SCHURMAN

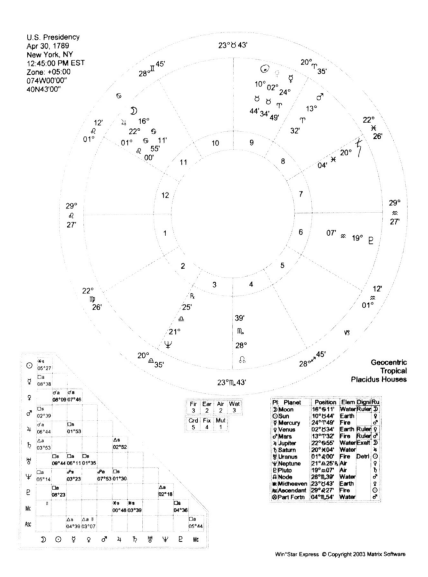

U.S. Presidency
Apr 30, 1789
New York, NY
12:45:00 PM EST
Zone: +05:00
074W00'00"
40N43'00"

Geocentric
Tropical
Placidus Houses

Fir	Ear	Air	Wat
3	2	2	3

Crd	Fix	Mut
5	4	1

Pl.	Planet	Position	Elem	Digni	Ru.
☽	Moon	16°♋11'	Water	Ruler	☽
☉	Sun	10°♉44'	Earth		♀
☿	Mercury	24°♈49'	Fire		♂
♀	Venus	02°♉34'	Earth	Ruler	♀
♂	Mars	13°♈32'	Fire	Ruler	♂
♃	Jupiter	22°♋55'	Water	Exalt	☽
♄	Saturn	20°♓04'	Water		♃
♅	Uranus	01°♌00'	Fire	Detri	☉
♆	Neptune	21°♎25' ℞	Air		♀
♇	Pluto	19°♒07'	Air		♄
☊	Node	28°♏39'	Water		♂
⚷	Midheaven	23°♉43'	Earth		♀
As	Ascendant	29°♌27'	Fire		☉
⊗	Part Fortn	04°♏54'	Water		♂

Win*Star Express © Copyright 2003 Matrix Software

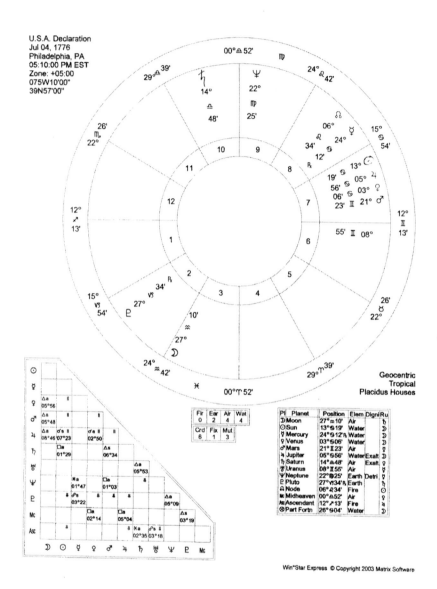

U.S.A. Declaration
Jul 04, 1776
Philadelphia, PA
05:10:00 PM EST
Zone: +05:00
075W10'00"
39N57'00"

Geocentric
Tropical
Placidus Houses

Fir	Ear	Air	Wat
0	2	4	4

Crd	Fix	Mut
6	1	3

Pl	Planet	Position	Elem	Digni	Ru
☽	Moon	27°≈10'	Air		♄
☉	Sun	13°♋19'	Water		☽
☿	Mercury	24°♋12'℞	Water		☽
♀	Venus	03°♋06'	Water		☽
♂	Mars	21°♊23'	Air		☿
♃	Jupiter	05°♋56'	Water	Exalt	☽
♄	Saturn	14°♎48'	Air	Exalt.	♀
♅	Uranus	08°♊55'	Air		☿
♆	Neptune	22°♍25'	Earth	Detri	☿
♇	Pluto	27°♑34'℞	Earth		♄
☊	Node	06°♌34'	Fire		☉
Ꝏ	Midheaven	00°♎52'	Air		♀
Asc	Ascendant	12°♐13'	Fire		♃
⊗	Part Fortn	26°♋04'	Water		☽

Win*Star Express © Copyright 2003 Matrix Software

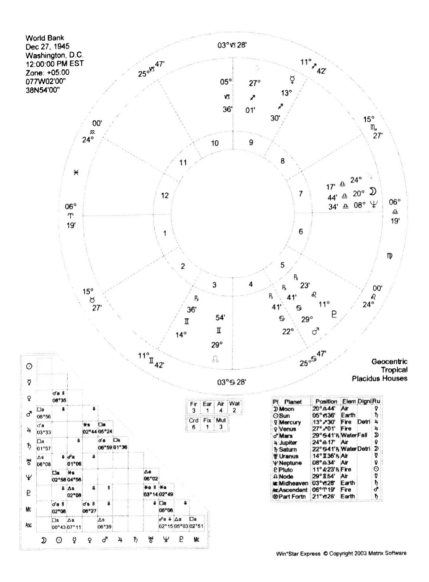

World Bank
Dec 27, 1945
Washington, D.C.
12:00:00 PM EST
Zone: +05:00
077W02'00"
38N54'00"

03°♑28'

25°♑47'   11°♐42'

05°   27°   ☿
♑   ♐   13°
36'   01'   ♐
                 30'

                                          15°
                                          ♏,
                                          27'

00'
♒
24'

✶

                              17' ♎ 24°
                              44' ♎ 20° ☽
                              34' ♎ 08° ♆   06°
                                                ♎
06°   19'
♈
19'

                                                ♍

15°   00'
♉   ♌
27'   24°

                              R̂   23'
                         R̂ 41' ♌
                  36'   41' ♋ 11°   ♇
                  ♊   ♋   29°
                  14°   22' ♂
                  ♊
                  29'
                  ♋

11°
♊42'   25°♋47'

03°♋28'

Geocentric
Tropical
Placidus Houses

	Fir	Ear	Air	Wat
	3	1	4	2
	Crd	Fix	Mut	
	6	1	3	

Pl	Planet	Position	Elem	Digni	Ru
☽	Moon	20°♎44'	Air		♀
☉	Sun	05°♑36'	Earth		♄
☿	Mercury	13°♐30'	Fire	Detri	♃
♀	Venus	27°♐01'	Fire		♃
♂	Mars	29°♋41'℞	Water	Fall	☽
♃	Jupiter	24°♊17'	Air		♀
♄	Saturn	22°♋41'℞	Water	Detri	☽
♅	Uranus	14°♊36'℞	Air		☿
♆	Neptune	08°♎34'	Air		♀
♇	Pluto	11°♌23'℞	Fire		☉
☊	Node	29°♊54'	Air		☿
Mc	Midheaven	03°♑28'	Earth		♄
As	Ascendant	06°♈19'	Fire		♂
⊛	Part Fortn	21°♑28'	Earth		♄

Win*Star Express © Copyright 2003 Matrix Software

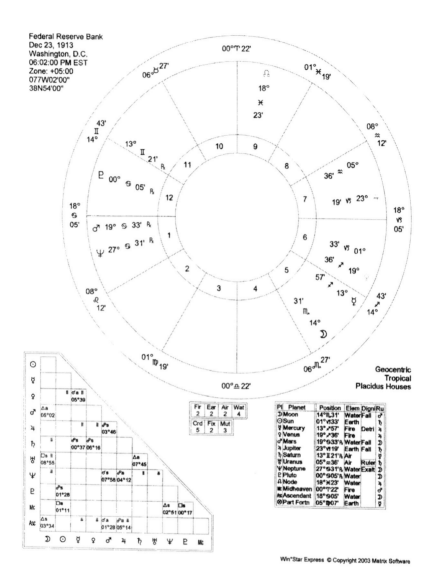

Federal Reserve Bank
Dec 23, 1913
Washington, D.C.
06:02:00 PM EST
Zone: +05:00
077W02'00"
38N54'00"

Geocentric
Tropical
Placidus Houses

Pl	Planet	Position	Elem	Digni	Ru
☽	Moon	14°♏31'	Water	Fall	♂
☉	Sun	01°♑33'	Earth		♄
☿	Mercury	13°♐57'	Fire	Detri	♃
♀	Venus	19°♐36'	Fire		♃
♂	Mars	19°♋33'℞	Water	Fall	☽
♃	Jupiter	23°♋19'	Earth	Fall	☽
♄	Saturn	13°♊21'℞	Air		☿
♅	Uranus	05°≈36'	Air	Ruler	♄
♆	Neptune	27°♋31'℞	Water	Exalt	☽
♇	Pluto	00°♋05'℞	Water		☽
☊	Node	18°♓23'	Water		♃
⚷	Midheaven	00°♈22'	Fire		♂
Asc	Ascendant	18°♋05'	Water		☽
⊕	Part Fortn	05°♍07'	Earth		☿

Fir	Ear	Air	Wat
2	2	2	4

Crd	Fix	Mut
5	2	3

Win*Star Express © Copyright 2003 Matrix Software

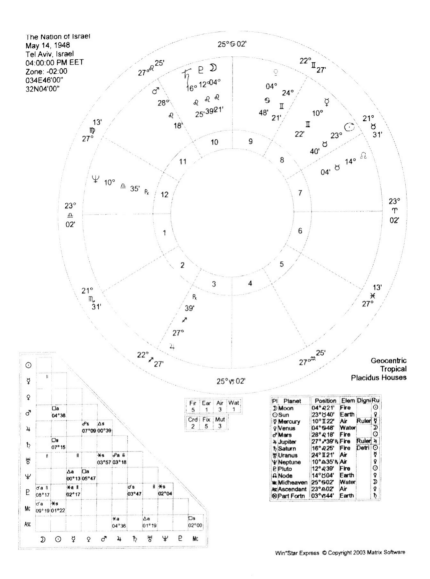

Geocentric
Tropical
Placidus Houses

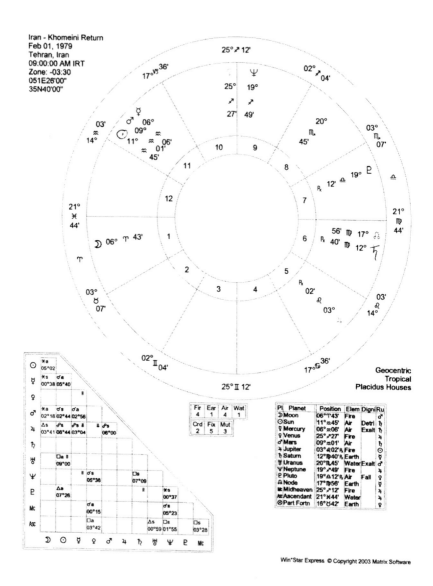

Iran - Khomeini Return
Feb 01, 1979
Tehran, Iran
09:00:00 AM IRT
Zone: -03:30
051E26'00"
35N40'00"

Geocentric
Tropical
Placidus Houses

Fir	Ear	Air	Wat
4	1	4	1

Crd	Fix	Mut
2	5	3

Pl	Planet	Position	Elem	Digni	Ru
☽	Moon	06°♈43'	Fire		♂
☉	Sun	11°♒45'	Air	Detri	♄
☿	Mercury	06°♒06'	Air	Exalt	♄
♀	Venus	25°♐27'	Fire		♃
♂	Mars	09°♒01'	Air		♄
♃	Jupiter	03°♌02'℞	Fire		☉
♄	Saturn	12°♍40'℞	Earth		☿
♅	Uranus	20°♏45'	Water	Exalt	♂
♆	Neptune	19°♐49'	Fire		♃
♇	Pluto	19°♎12'℞	Air	Fall	♀
☊	Node	17°♍56'℞	Earth		☿
⊼	Midheaven	25°♐12'	Fire		♃
Asc	Ascendant	21°♓44'	Water		♃
⊗	Part Fortn	16°♉42'	Earth		♀

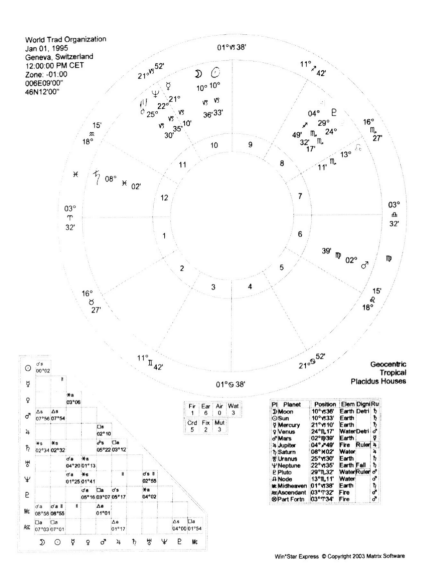

World Trad Organization
Jan 01, 1995
Geneva, Switzerland
12:00:00 PM CET
Zone: -01:00
006E09'00"
46N12'00"

Geocentric
Tropical
Placidus Houses

Fir	Ear	Air	Wat
1	6	0	3

Crd	Fix	Mut
5	2	3

Pl	Planet	Position	Elem	Digni	Ru
☽	Moon	10°ᴠ36'	Earth	Detri	♄
☉	Sun	10°ᴠ33'	Earth		♄
☿	Mercury	21°ᴠ10'	Earth		♄
♀	Venus	24°♏17'	Water	Detri	♂
♂	Mars	02°♍39'	Earth		☿
♃	Jupiter	04°♐49'	Fire	Ruler	♃
♄	Saturn	08°♓02'	Water		♃
♅	Uranus	25°ᴠ30'	Earth		♄
♇	Pluto	29°♏32'	Water	Ruler	♂
☊	Node	13°♏11'	Water		♂
⯝	Midheaven	01°ᴠ38'	Earth		♄
Aꜱ	Ascendant	03°♈32'	Fire		♂
⊗	Part Fortn	03°♈34'	Fire		♂

Win*Star Express © Copyright 2003 Matrix Software

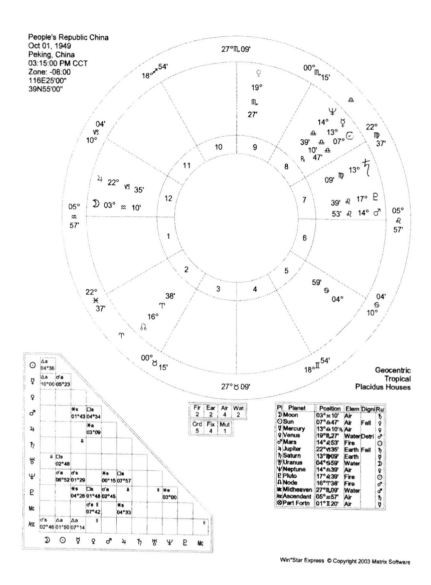

Win*Star Express © Copyright 2003 Matrix Software

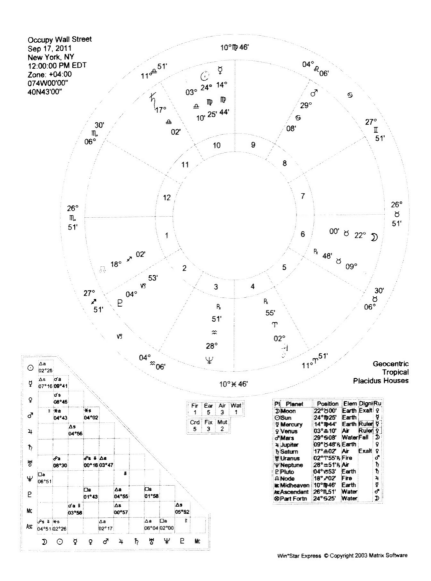

Occupy Wall Street
Sep 17, 2011
New York, NY
12:00:00 PM EDT
Zone: +04:00
074W00'00"
40N43'00"

10° ♍ 46'

11° ♎ 51'

03° 24° 14'
♎ ♍ ♍
10' 25' 44'

04° ♌ 06'

♂
29°
♋
08'

27°
♊
51'

30'
♏
06'

♄
17°
♎
02'

10   9

11   8

12   7

1   6

26°
♏
51'

26°
♉
51'

00° ♉ 22° ☽

18° ♐ 02'

R 48' ♉
09°

27°
♐
51'

04° ♑ 53'

♇

2   5

3   4

R
51'

R
55'

♈
02°

30'
♉
06'

♒
28°
♅

04° ♒ 06'

10° ♓ 46'

11° ♈ 51'

Geocentric
Tropical
Placidus Houses

Fir	Ear	Air	Wat
1	5	3	1

Crd	Fix	Mut
5	3	2

Pl	Planet	Position	Elem	Digni	Ru
☽	Moon	22°♉00'	Earth	Exalt	♀
☉	Sun	24°♍25'	Earth		☿
☿	Mercury	14°♍44'	Earth	Ruler	☿
♀	Venus	03°♎10'	Air	Ruler	♀
♂	Mars	29°♋08'	Water	Fall	☽
♃	Jupiter	09°♉48'R	Earth		♀
♄	Saturn	17°♎02'	Air	Exalt	♀
♅	Uranus	02°♈55'R	Fire		♂
♆	Neptune	28°♒51'R	Air		♄
♇	Pluto	04°♑53'	Earth		♄
☊	Node	18°♐02'	Fire		♃
⚸	Midheaven	10°♍46'	Earth		☿
Asc	Ascendant	26°♏51'	Water		♂
⊕	Part Fortn	24°♋25'	Water		☽

		☽	☉	☿	♀	♂	♃	♄	♅	♆	♇	Mc
☉	△a 02°25											
☿	△s 07°16	♂a 09°41										
♀	□s 08°45											
♂	‖a 04°43	✶s 04°02										
♃		△s 04°56										
♄												
♅	♂a 08°30		♂s △a 00°16 03°47									
♆	□a 06°51											
♇			□a 01°43	△a 04°55	□s 01°58							
Mc		♂a 03°58		△s 00°57							△s 05°52	
Asc	♂s ‖s 04°51 02°26			△a 02°17		△a □a 06°04 02°00	‖					

| | ☽ | ☉ | ☿ | ♀ | ♂ | ♃ | ♄ | ♅ | ♆ | ♇ | Mc |

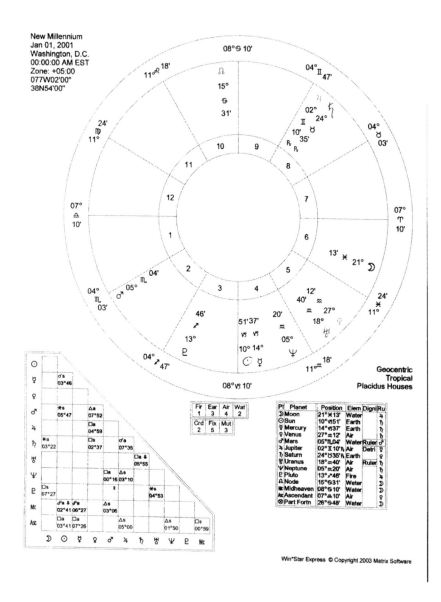

New Millennium
Jan 01, 2001
Washington, D.C.
00:00:00 AM EST
Zone: +05:00
077W02'00"
38N54'00"

08°♋10'

11°♌18'

04°♊47'

15°
♋
31'

02°♊24'♄
10'♂
10'
R 35'
R

04°♉
03'

10   9

11   8

07°
♎
10'

12

7

07°
♈
10'

1

6

13'✳21'☽

04°♏
03'

05°♏04'

2

5

12'
40'♒
♒27'
18'♀
♓
c

24°
♓
11'

46'
✶
13'

3   4

51'37'
♑ ♑

20'

05°

18°♒

04°♐47'
♇

10° 14'
☉☿

18'
♒

08°♑10'

Geocentric
Tropical
Placidus Houses

Fir	Ear	Air	Wat
1	3	4	2
Crd	Fix	Mut	
2	5	3	

Pl	Planet	Position	Elem	Digni	Ru
☽	Moon	21°♓13'	Water		♃
☉	Sun	10°♑51'	Earth		♄
☿	Mercury	14°♑37'	Earth		♄
♀	Venus	27°♒12'	Air		♄
♂	Mars	05°♏04'	Water	Ruler	♂
♃	Jupiter	02°♊10'R	Air	Detri	☿
♄	Saturn	24°♉35'R	Earth		♀
♅	Uranus	18°♒40'	Air	Ruler	♄
♆	Neptune	05°♒20'	Air		♄
♇	Pluto	13°♐46'	Fire		♃
☊	Node	15°♋31'	Water		☽
⚸	Midheaven	08°♋10'	Water		☽
As	Ascendant	07°♎10'	Air		♀
⊕	Part Fortn	26°♋48'	Water		☽

☉										
☿	♂s 03°46									
♀										
♂	✳s 05°47	△a 07°52								
♃		□s 04°59								
♄	✶a 03°22	□s 02°37	♂a 07°35							
♅			□a 05°55							
♆			□a 00°16 03°10	△s						
♇	□s 07°27		ı	✶s 04°53						
Mc	♂a ♀a 02°41 06°27	△s 03°06								
Asc	□a □a 03°41 07°26		△s 05°00		△s 01°50	□s 00°59				
	☽	☉	☿	♀	♂	♃	♄	♅	♆	♇	Mc

Win*Star Express © Copyright 2003 Matrix Software

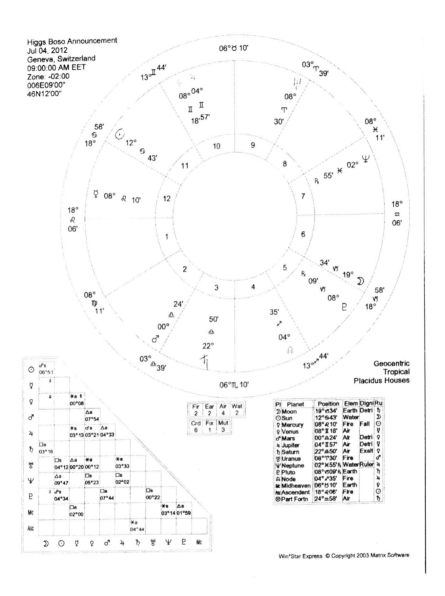

Higgs Boso Announcement
Jul 04, 2012
Geneva, Switzerland
09:00:00 AM EET
Zone: -02:00
006E09'00"
46N12'00"

Geocentric
Tropical
Placidus Houses

Fir	Ear	Air	Wat
2	2	4	2

Crd	Fix	Mut
6	1	3

Pl	Planet	Position	Elem	Digni	Ru
☽	Moon	19°ⅤⅤ34'	Earth	Detri	♄
☉	Sun	12°♋43'	Water		☽
☿	Mercury	08°♌10'	Fire	Fall	☉
♀	Venus	08°Ⅱ18'	Air		☿
♂	Mars	00°♎24'	Air	Detri	♀
♃	Jupiter	04°Ⅱ57'	Air	Detri	☿
♄	Saturn	22°♎50'	Air	Exalt	♀
♅	Uranus	08°♈30'	Fire		♂
♆	Neptune	02°♓55'R	Water	Ruler	♃
♇	Pluto	08°ⅤⅤ09'R	Earth		♄
☊	Node	04°♐35'	Fire		♃
⚷	Midheaven	06°♉10'	Earth		♀
Asc	Ascendant	18°♌06'	Fire		☉
⊗	Part Fortn	24°♒58'	Air		♄

Win*Star Express © Copyright 2003 Matrix Software

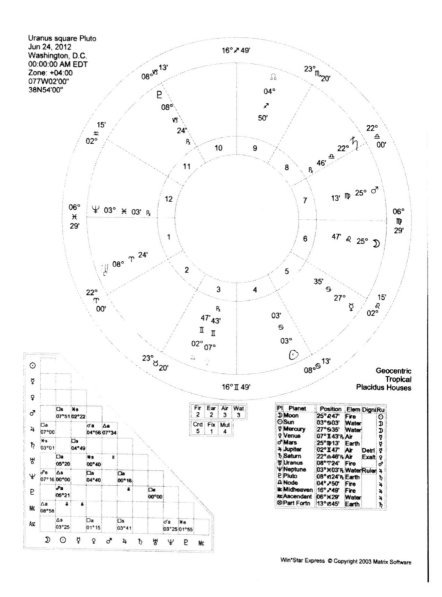

Uranus square Pluto
Jun 24, 2012
Washington, D.C.
00:00:00 AM EDT
Zone: +04:00
077W02'00"
38N54'00"

Geocentric
Tropical
Placidus Houses

Fir	Ear	Air	Wat
2	2	3	3

Crd	Fix	Mut
5	1	4

Pl	Planet	Position	Elem	Digni	Ru
☽	Moon	25°♌47'	Fire		☉
☉	Sun	03°♋03'	Water		☽
☿	Mercury	27°♋35'	Water		☿
♀	Venus	07°Ⅱ43'℞	Air		☿
♂	Mars	25°♍13'	Earth		☿
♃	Jupiter	02°♎47'	Air	Detri	♀
♄	Saturn	22°♎46'℞	Air	Exalt	♂
♅	Uranus	08°♈24'	Fire		♂
♆	Neptune	03°♓03'℞	Water	Ruler	♃
♇	Pluto	08°♑24'℞	Earth		♄
☊	Node	04°♐50'	Fire		♃
✶	Midheaven	16°♐49'	Fire		♃
✶	Ascendant	06°♓29'	Water		♃
⊕	Part Fortn	13°♑45'	Earth		♄

Win*Star Express © Copyright 2003 Matrix Software

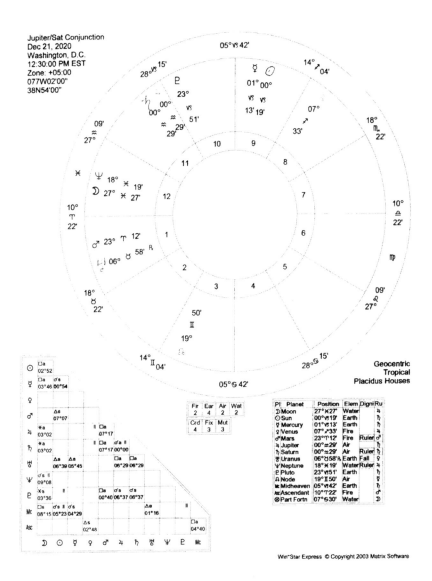

Jupiter/Sat Conjunction
Dec 21, 2020
Washington, D.C.
12:30:00 PM EST
Zone: +05:00
077W02'00"
38N54'00"

Geocentric
Tropical
Placidus Houses

	Fir	Ear	Air	Wat
	2	4	2	2
	Crd	Fix	Mut	
	4	3	3	

Pl	Planet	Position	Elem	Digni	Ru
☽	Moon	27°♓27'	Water		♃
☉	Sun	00°♑19'	Earth		♄
☿	Mercury	01°♑13'	Earth		♄
♀	Venus	07°♐33'	Fire		♃
♂	Mars	23°♈12'	Fire	Ruler	♂
♃	Jupiter	00°♒29'	Air		♄
♄	Saturn	00°♒29'	Air	Ruler	♄
♅	Uranus	06°♉58'R	Earth	Fall	♀
♆	Neptune	18°♓19'	Water	Ruler	♃
♇	Pluto	23°♑51'	Earth		♄
☊	Node	19°♊50'	Air		☿
Ⅰ☽	Midheaven	05°♑42'	Earth		♄
Asc	Ascendant	10°♈22'	Fire		♂
⊗	Part Fortn	07°♋30'	Water		☽

Win*Star Express © Copyright 2003 Matrix Software

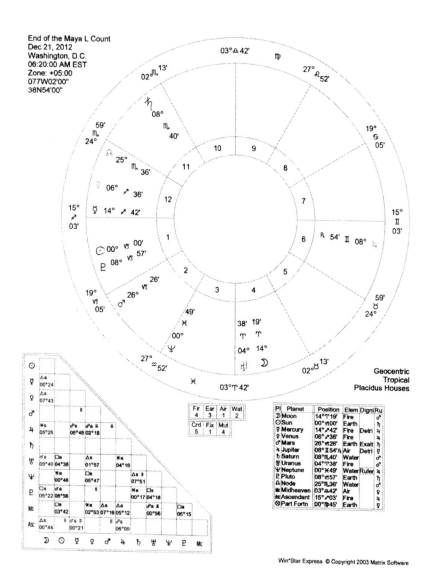

End of the Maya L Count
Dec 21, 2012
Washington, D.C.
06:20:00 AM EST
Zone: +05:00
077W02'00"
38N54'00"

Geocentric
Tropical
Placidus Houses

Fir	Ear	Air	Wat
4	3	1	2

Crd	Fix	Mut
5	1	4

Pl	Planet	Position	Elem	Digni	Ru
☽	Moon	14°♈19'	Fire		♂
☉	Sun	00°♑00'	Earth		♄
☿	Mercury	14°♐42'	Fire	Detri	♃
♀	Venus	06°♐36'	Fire		♃
♂	Mars	26°♑26'	Earth	Exalt	♄
♃	Jupiter	08°♊54'R	Air	Detri	☿
♄	Saturn	08°♏40'	Water		♂
♅	Uranus	04°♈38'	Fire		♂
♆	Neptune	00°♓49'	Water	Ruler	♃
♇	Pluto	08°♑57'	Earth		♄
☊	Node	25°♏36'	Water		♂
⚷	Midheaven	03°♎42'	Air		♀
Asc	Ascendant	15°♐03'	Fire		♃
⊗	Part Fortn	00°♍45'	Earth		☿

Win*Star Express © Copyright 2003 Matrix Software

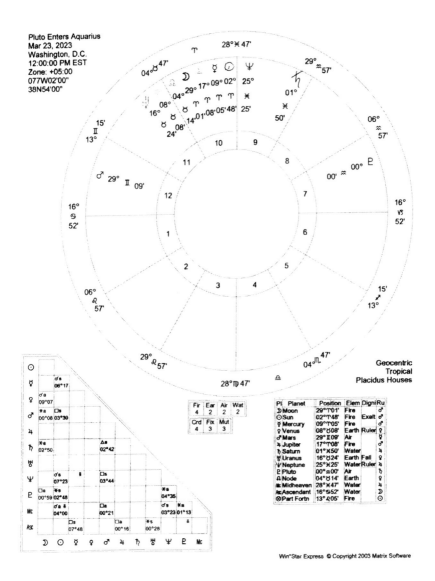

Pluto Enters Aquarius
Mar 23, 2023
Washington, D.C.
12:00:00 PM EST
Zone: +05:00
077W02'00"
38N54'00"

Geocentric
Tropical
Placidus Houses

Fir	Ear	Air	Wat
4	2	2	2

Crd	Fix	Mut
4	3	3

Pl	Planet	Position	Elem	Digni	Ru
☽	Moon	29°♈01'	Fire		♂
☉	Sun	02°♈48'	Fire	Exalt	♂
☿	Mercury	09°♈05'	Fire		☿
♀	Venus	08°♉08'	Earth	Ruler	♀
♂	Mars	29°♊09'	Air		☿
♃	Jupiter	17°♈08'	Fire		♂
♄	Saturn	01°♓50'	Water		♃
♅	Uranus	16°♉24'	Earth	Fall	♀
♆	Neptune	25°♓25'	Water	Ruler	♃
♇	Pluto	00°♒00'	Air		♄
☊	Node	04°♉14'	Earth		♀
Ⓜ	Midheaven	28°♓47'	Water		♃
Asc	Ascendant	16°♋52'	Water		☽
⊗	Part Fortn	13°♌05'	Fire		☉

Win*Star Express © Copyright 2003 Matrix Software

89

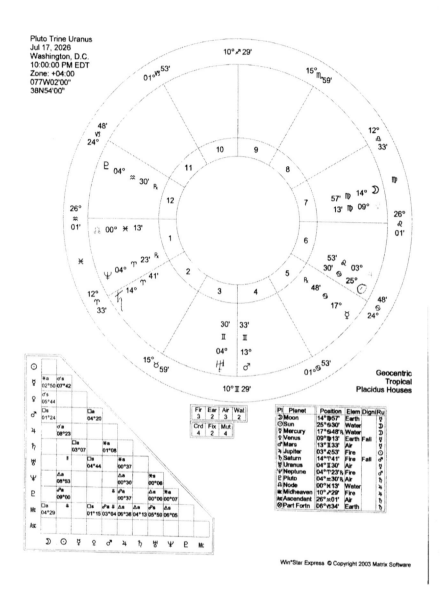

Pluto Trine Uranus
Jul 17, 2026
Washington, D.C.
10:00:00 PM EDT
Zone: +04:00
077W02'00"
38N54'00"

Geocentric
Tropical
Placidus Houses

Fir	Ear	Air	Wat
3	2	3	2

Crd	Fix	Mut
4	2	4

Pl	Planet	Position	Elem	Digni	Ru
☽	Moon	14°♍57'	Earth		☿
☉	Sun	25°♋30'	Water		☽
☿	Mercury	17°♋48' R	Water		☽
♀	Venus	09°♍13'	Earth	Fall	☿
♂	Mars	13°♊33'	Air		☿
♃	Jupiter	03°♌53'	Fire		☉
♄	Saturn	14°♈41'	Fire	Fall	♂
♅	Uranus	04°♊30'	Air		☿
♆	Neptune	04°♈23' R	Fire		♂
♇	Pluto	04°♒30' R	Air		♄
☊	Node	00°♓13'	Water		♃
⚷	Midheaven	10°♐29'	Fire		♃
Asc	Ascendant	26°♒01'	Air		♄
⊕	Part Fortn	06°♑34'	Earth		♄

Win*Star Express © Copyright 2003 Matrix Software

CPSIA information can be obtained at www.ICGtesting.com
Printed in the USA
BVOW020504210113

310982BV00007B/20/P